剑桥双语分级阅读·小说馆（第2版）

■ 原版系列编辑 Philip Prowse



# But Was It Murder? 死亡诊断

[英] 贾尼亚·巴雷尔 著
黄德利 编译

北京语言大学出版社
BEIJING LANGUAGE AND CULTURE UNIVERSITY PRESS

CAMBRIDGE UNIVERSITY PRESS

社图号25019



**图书在版编目（CIP）数据**

死亡诊断 ： 英汉对照 / （英）贾尼亚·巴雷尔（Jania Barrell）著 ； 黄德利编译. -- 2版. -- 北京 ： 北京语言大学出版社, 2025. 3. --（剑桥双语分级阅读小说馆）. -- ISBN 978-7-5619-6738-6

Ⅰ. H319.4

中国国家版本馆CIP数据核字第2025CH1506号

**死亡诊断**
SIWANG ZHENDUAN

**责任编辑：** 孙冠群
**责任印制：** 周 燚

**出版发行：** 北京语言大学出版社
**社　　址：** 北京市海淀区学院路 15 号，100083
**网　　址：** www.blcup.com
**电子信箱：** service@blcup.com
**电　　话：** 编 辑 部 010-8230 1019
发 行 部 010-8230 3650/3591/3648
北语书店 010-8230 3653
网购咨询 010-8230 3908
**印　　刷：** 东港股份有限公司

**版　　次：** 2017 年 6 月第 1 版　2025 年 3 月第 2 版　**印　　次：** 2025 年 3 月第 1 次印刷
**开　　本：** 880 毫米 × 1230 毫米　1/32　**印　　张：** 6.375
**字　　数：** 150 千字　**定　　价：** 23.00 元

PRINTED IN CHINA
**凡有印装质量问题，本社负责调换。售后QQ号1367565611，电话010-82303590**

# Preface

# 前言

“剑桥双语分级阅读·小说馆”是一套从剑桥大学出版社引进的面向非英语国家英语学习者的分级系列读物，由英语语言教学专家及小说作家合力创作。创作过程历时三十余年，出版后受到世界各地英语教师和英语学习者的喜爱，许多读本再版多次，三十余年来畅销不衰，成为受全球英语学习者青睐的优秀读本。

本系列读物具有以下突出特色：

1. 是原创英语读物，而非改编自普通作品的读物。因此，阅读本系列读物，我们读到的是原汁原味的原创英语，而非人为改编过的二手英语。

2. 是当代优秀短篇小说，而非年代久远的小说。因此，阅读本系列读物，我们读到的是当今鲜活的、学了就能用的英语，而非穿越时空的、学了用不上的英语；了解的是与读者同时代不同国家人们的生活和思想，而非隔代人的生活、文化和风土人情。

3. 是专为非英语国家的英语学习者量身定制的读物，而非为英语母语者所写的大众读物。因此，本系列读物是中国读者首选的英语学习读物。

4. 是英美知名小说家和英语语言教学专家合力创作的读物。小说家保障了读物的可读性与可欣赏性，英语语言教学专家保障了读物语言作为英语习得材料的科学性与可学性。本系列读物中的多个读本都曾在世界上颇具影响力的“语言学习者文学奖”（Language Learner Literature Award）评选中获得大奖。因此，阅读本系列读物，我们会在欣赏小说的同时，自然而然地、有效地提高自己的英语水平。

5. 本系列读物的故事题材丰富多样，包括侦探、情感、历险、悬疑、人文、科幻、喜剧等，读者可以随心选择自己喜欢的类别阅读；故事内容生动有趣，故事情节引人入胜、扣人心弦，读者一旦开始阅读，就想一口气读完，使阅读真正升华到“悦读”。

6. 随书附赠的音频材料内容精彩，是专业配音员的演绎再创作。听着它，我们犹如在听广播剧、听评书，又仿佛是在听电影、听话剧……这种聆听英语的享受将彻底扫除学生对英语听力的畏难心理。

7. 本系列读物所使用的语言，既有英式英语，也有美式英语，对应的音频材料也相应分为英音和美音，读者可根据自己的喜好来选择。

8. 本系列近百本读物根据《欧洲语言共同参考框架》(CEFR)和剑桥大学外语考评部开发的 ESOL 考试的标准来确定级别划分，是建立在科学研究和实践基础之上的分级。全套共分七个级别（与中国学生英语基础水平的大致对应关系，请参见图书封底表格），读者可根据自己的英语基础选择相应级别的读本来学习。

为了更好地帮助中国学生学习和欣赏，“剑桥双语分级阅读·小说馆”从剑桥大学出版社原版引进后又增加了以下内容：

1. 增加了适量的辅助学习内容，包括“读前思考”“读后活动”“学习指导”三个板块，其中“学习指导”板块又包括生词、短语和表达、文化点滴、阅读练习四项内容。增加这些板块的目的是全方位帮助学生提升英语阅读能力，扩充词汇量，扫除阅读中的文化障碍，增强对英语小说的鉴赏能力。

2. 增加了小说全文的参考译文。出于语言学习的考虑，译文多采用直译，但也尽量符合中文的表达习惯。

值得一提的是，所增加的辅助学习内容和参考译文，全部由来自全国不同省市知名中学（包括人大附中、北大附中、清华附中、黄冈中学、上海中学等三十余所中学）的一线英语教师完成。这些一线教师的加盟，确保了所加内容与中国学生的英语学习特点和学习需求相吻合，为学生阅读和欣赏读物、提高英语水平给予恰到好处的助力。

英语阅读是英语课堂的延伸和补充，也是培养英语语感、提高英语水平的有效途径。选择一套好的英语读物，收获的将不仅仅是语言的进步。欢迎年轻朋友们来到“剑桥双语分级阅读·小说馆”，打开一本本好书，品味一个个好故事，为实现梦想搭建桥梁。

北京语言大学出版社

# Contents 目录

# People in the story

## 故事中的人物

**Detective Inspector Rod Eliot:** Policemen at New Cross police station, London

**刑侦督察罗德·埃利奥特：**伦敦新十字警察局的警察

**Detective Constable Jamie Bowen:** Policemen at New Cross police station, London

**刑侦警员杰米·鲍恩：**伦敦新十字警察局的警察

**Police Constable Drewitt:** Policemen at New Cross police station, London

**警员德鲁伊特：**伦敦新十字警察局的警察

**Sally Eliot:** Rod Eliot's wife

**萨莉·埃利奥特：**罗德·埃利奥特的妻子

**Micky Eliot:** Rod Eliot's son

**米基·埃利奥特：**罗德·埃利奥特的儿子

**Alex Forley:** Owner of an antique furniture shop

亚历克斯·福尔利：一家古董家具店的老板

**Mr and Mrs Crowther:** Forley's neighbours

克劳瑟先生及太太：福尔利的邻居

**Amanda Grant:** Forley's girlfriend

阿曼达·格兰特：福尔利的女朋友

**Philip Wilver:** Forley's doctor

菲利普·维尔弗：福尔利的医生

**Lisa Wilver:** Philip Wilver's wife

莉萨·维尔弗：菲利普·维尔弗的妻子

**Mrs Brook:** A cleaner

布鲁克太太：一位保洁工

**Linda Scott:** Manager of Forley's antique furniture shop

琳达·斯科特：福尔利古董家具店的经理

# Before reading

## 读前思考

1. Look at the front cover and read the blurb on the back cover. What sort of story is this?
2. Read the contents on page 1. Say what you think will happen in the story.
3. If you have the recording, listen to Chapter 1.

## Chapter 1
# Missing The Queen's Head

Detective Inspector Rod Eliot was watching the rain running down his office window. He looked at his watch. 6:30. Time to leave the mountain of papers on his desk and go to The Queen's Head pub across the road.

'But only one beer,' he told himself. 'I don't want to be stopped by some junior policeman for drunk driving. Then I'll have to go home to an empty house.'

Just as he was leaving the office, the phone rang. He turned back automatically and picked it up. He half hoped it might be his wife.

'Sorry to disturb you, sir,' said Detective Constable Jamie Bowen. 'But we've got a bit of a problem.'

'So have I,' said Eliot. 'I shouldn't be here. Ask Inspector Merryon.'

'Sorry, sir,' said Bowen, 'but Inspector Merryon hasn't arrived yet. He phoned to say his car is stuck in a traffic jam in Hackney. He probably won't be here for at least an hour.'

Eliot hit the top of his desk angrily. The lights from The Queen's Head looked so inviting. But in the street below people were crowded into shop doorways, trying to escape from the rain. The water poured onto the street and was thrown up again by the lines of cars moving slowly away from the centre of London.

'All right, Bowen,' he said. 'You'd better tell me about it then. What is it?'

'We've just had a report of a death, sir. And there's a gun.'

This was the last thing Eliot wanted to hear. He had been in a bad mood all day. He usually liked Friday because of the weekend ahead, when he could spend time with his wife Sally and eight-year-old son Micky. Micky was crazy about football, and Eliot always took him to watch West Ham on Saturdays when they played at home. This weekend would be different, though. Eliot had to work, and Sally had taken Micky to her parents' house in Brighton for two nights. He had argued with her that morning.

'Stop shouting,' she had said. 'You're just angry because you don't want us to go away. Why can't you admit it?'

She was right, but knowing this only made him more angry. He had left the house without saying goodbye to her.

He had tried to ring several times to say sorry, but there was no answer. Now she would be at her parents' house. And she could not speak to him openly there because they would be listening.

'I knew this would be a bad day from the moment I woke up,' he told Bowen. 'All right. We'll have to go. Where is it?'

'Blackheath, I'm afraid, sir.'

Eliot sighed. Blackheath was only six kilometres from New Cross police station. But at this time on a Friday night there was so much traffic that the journey could take over an hour.

Eliot could not think of a worse way of spending Friday evening, especially as he had to be in his office early next morning. Why did everyone try to leave London at the same time? One day the whole city would be stuck in one big traffic jam. Already the traffic moved more slowly than it had a hundred years ago. It was madness.

'Meet me downstairs in ten minutes, Bowen,' he said. 'Oh, and there'll have to be medical reports. Check that someone's told a doctor and the pathologist.'

Eliot turned away from the window. Well, at least Sally and Micky weren't waiting for him at home. He had better phone them now. It might be his last chance this evening.

Sally's father picked up the phone. 'Hello Rod. Pity you can't be here. The weather's beautiful. How's the job?'

Eliot made himself chat politely for a few minutes and then asked to speak to Sally.

'I'm afraid she's not here,' her father said. 'She's taken Micky for a walk. He couldn't wait to see the sea. Any message for her?' Eliot couldn't believe his bad luck.

'Just say I'm pleased they've arrived safely,' he said. 'And give her my love. I'll ring again tomorrow.'

He put down the phone and took one last look at The Queen's Head. The traffic seemed hardly to have moved. Well, at least he could get Bowen to drive.

## Chapter 2

# The colour of death

The car went forward a few metres, and then stopped again. At first Bowen had switched on the blue light and siren so that other drivers would let them pass. But there was no space for them to get through, and they had almost caused two accidents.

They were nearly in Blackheath now. The rain had stopped, but the traffic seemed to be getting worse.

Blackheath Village is one of the prettiest and greenest parts of southeast London. Its narrow streets are on a hill with pleasant views, unusual houses and many restaurants. Large areas of grass separate the village from the main road. Here children play and lovers wander, and families walk with their dogs.

Tomorrow night there would be crowds, as it was November 5, Guy Fawkes Day. Thousands of people would come to the Blackheath firework show if they weren't having parties in their own gardens. Some of these parties seemed to have started already. The sky was full of the sounds and colours of fireworks exploding above their heads.

Eliot thought about his son with a sudden pain. Micky would be so excited tomorrow. Eliot would have loved to bring him here.

He made himself think about his work instead.

'What do you know about this death?' he asked Bowen.

'Not much, sir. It's a white man in his thirties.'

'I suppose we'll find out more when we arrive. If we ever do arrive, Bowen,' added Eliot impatiently.

'Sorry, sir. I'm doing my best,' said Bowen.

Eliot wondered how Bowen would feel about seeing the dead body. It was never easy, even for himself after all these years, though he had become much harder.

Bowen was twenty-eight, ten years younger than Eliot, and had worked with him since first joining the police. His parents were rich and he had been to Cambridge University. This had worried Eliot at first. But Bowen was honest and intelligent and a good policeman. Eliot now had a high opinion of him, though he did not often show it.

But there was one thing about Bowen which Eliot could not understand: he was always falling in love with the wrong women. They were either married, or not interested in him, or totally crazy. Recently he had started asking Eliot for advice when they were in the car together.

'All that education, and he can't get a girlfriend. What a waste!' Eliot thought. 'And he's not bad looking, with those dark eyes and all that black curly hair.'

Eliot knew how lucky he was to be happily married himself. He was sorry for Bowen and angry with himself for arguing with Sally that morning. He wished she had been there when he phoned.

At last they turned off the main road and stopped outside a small but beautiful eighteenth century house at the end of a quiet street. Lights were shining from all the windows. Eliot got out and stretched his legs. Normally he would have looked forward to seeing the inside of such a lovely building.

A young policeman opened the door. He looked pale, and seemed very pleased to see them.

'Evening, sir. Evening, sir,' he said, looking at each of them. 'My name's Drewitt. The, er, body's through here.'

They followed him through a hall with a deep red Persian carpet, past some beautiful wooden stairs and into a sitting room at the back. A fire was burning in the fireplace, and lamps on low tables threw a warm light over the curtains and walls and antique furniture. An open piano stood by the window, with music on it and a half-filled glass of red wine.

Eliot's attention was caught by a dark shape on the wall beside one of the armchairs. It was the same colour as the carpet in the hall. At first it seemed the only ugly thing in the room. But then Eliot looked down at the chair. He quickly looked away again.

It was a man's body. But he only knew it was a man from its shape and the clothes it wore. Not enough of the face remained to show what sex it had been. It sat in a chair with its back to the window. A gun lay beside it on the floor.

Eliot made himself look again. The hands were long, with thin, well-shaped fingers. Piano-playing hands. There was a thick gold ring on the third finger of the right hand. So he wasn't married, though he could be divorced. His clothes looked expensive, as you would expect in a house like this.

In the few seconds it took for these thoughts to cross Eliot's mind. Bowen had taken out his notebook and started questioning Drewitt.

'Bowen's becoming as hard as me,' Eliot thought. 'Not like young Drewitt there. He's as white as a sheet.'

'Any idea who he is?' Bowen asked Drewitt.

Drewitt was obviously having difficulty speaking.

'Well, sir,' he said at last, 'the house belongs to a Mr Alex Forley. His neighbours called us. Mr and Mrs Crowther. They live next door. He normally had tea with them on Fridays, and they got worried when he didn't come this afternoon as he'd been feeling ill. He didn't answer his doorbell, so they got into the back garden and saw him through the window. The doctor's already been and gone, sir.'

'Yes,' said Bowen. 'He wouldn't have needed to stay long. Anyone can see the man's dead.'

'We'll have a word with the Crowthers later,' Eliot said. 'I'd better wait here till the pathologist arrives. Bowen, why don't you talk to the other neighbours? See if they can tell us anything interesting.'

There was a ring at the doorbell. Two more policemen came in and started taking photographs of the dead body, but it was another half hour before the pathologist arrived. He was a short fat cheerful man, who looked as if nothing could annoy him.

'Hello, Eliot. Good to see you again. Sorry it's taken me so long to get here. The traffic's awful. I expect it's all these Guy Fawkes Night parties. I don't see why they can't wait till tomorrow. But still, there's a bright side to everything. I managed to hear all of

Mahler's Eighth Symphony on the way here. A great recording. Life's too short to worry. Don't you agree, Eliot?'

Eliot did not answer.

'I'm sure *he*'d agree with me, if he could,' the pathologist said cheerfully, pointing to the body on the chair. 'Unless, of course, it was suicide. Well, I'd better take a look at him. I don't expect you want to stay here all night chatting.'

He opened his bag, and Eliot decided to go outside.

# Chapter 3
# Just friends

Eliot walked around the house. The garden was well cared for. He could see that even in the dark. The grass was cut, late roses were flowering on two walls, and the stone paths were clean and tidy. The windows of the sitting room were French windows, which opened like doors on to the garden outside.

'A lovely room. Perfect in summer,' he thought.

Automatically, he went up to the French windows and tried to open them. He was quite surprised to find they were unlocked.

'I suppose this is how Drewitt got in,' he thought. 'I wonder why they're open, though. It hasn't been the sort of weather for enjoying the garden. But it probably doesn't mean anything. Some people like to go out in all weathers to look at their roses.' He saw there was a gate in the back wall of the garden, which looked new. Sally wanted one of those in their own garden, so that they did not have to carry plants through the house.

He went back inside and looked in every room. The bathroom told him immediately that Forley lived alone.

One toothbrush stood in a mug next to a shaving brush, and there was a single towel in a ring on one wall. Eliot could see the letters AF on one corner. The other rooms were all as beautifully arranged as the sitting room. Forley obviously cared about his house very much, more than many single men.

'A man with a lot of taste and a lot of money,' Eliot thought. 'A lucky man. Except that his luck stopped today. I wonder what other people thought of his luck.'

He went downstairs and waited till the pathologist had finished his work.

'Can you tell me anything yet?' he asked him.

'Well, I don't think he's been dead very long. But I can't say any more until I've examined him properly. And I don't think you'll get the report until Monday. I couldn't tell you what time, I'm afraid. We're so busy at the moment. The work's increasing, and they're cutting the number of staff. The world's going mad. But I know you won't mind waiting, Eliot. You're a family man, aren't you? You'll have much more pleasant things to think about at the weekend.'

He went out of the door with a smile, just as Bowen walked in.

'Did you find out anything interesting?' Eliot asked.

'Not really, sir,' said Bowen. 'A lot of people were out. The ones I spoke to have all moved here quite recently, and don't seem to know anything about him. A few people mentioned they had sometimes seen a woman here, but no-one was very interested in him. None of them know what work he did.'

'City people!' said Eliot. 'They don't care about their neighbours. If Mr and Mrs Crowther hadn't called us, he could have been lying there for weeks before anyone noticed something was wrong. Well, we'd better go round and see them now.'

Number 20 was not as beautiful as Forley's house, Eliot thought. But there were roses growing around the front door and the front garden was bigger than Eliot's own. If he was offered a house like this, he would certainly not refuse. They walked up the path and rang the bell, paying no attention to the explosions of fireworks around them.

Mr Crowther opened the door immediately. He was a white-haired man in late middle age. He stood very straight, which made him seem taller than he really was. His face was lined, but he looked strong and healthy, though his hands were shaking.

'What happened to poor Alex?' he asked.

'We don't know yet, sir,' said Eliot. 'But we'd like to ask you and your wife some questions.'

Crowther controlled himself with an effort, and led them into a large sitting room. Eliot's attention was caught by the pictures which covered one of the walls. They were an interesting mix of colours, mostly blues and greens, and had obviously been painted by the same person. Mr Crowther introduced his wife, Catherine, and Eliot felt immediately that she was the painter.

She was a beautiful woman with blonde hair and lovely green eyes. It was difficult to tell her age, but she was certainly much younger than her husband. Eliot guessed she was in her forties. There was no colour in her face, but she answered his questions calmly enough. A strong and intelligent woman, Eliot thought.

'No, Inspector, we haven't seen Alex since a week ago,' she told him. 'We usually meet on Friday afternoons, either here or at his house. We've done it for years. He phoned this morning from his shop in Greenwich to say he was coming. He and I were going to play some music together. We often do that. It's a pleasant way to end the week.'

'I'm sure it is,' said Eliot, remembering his own

Friday afternoons. He turned to her husband.

'Have you known Mr Forley a long time, sir?'

'Let me see. It must be about fifteen years now, since he moved here. That was about a year after he left university. His mother had just died. She had a lot of money, and she left it all to Alex. Her death made him a very rich young man.'

'I see,' said Eliot. He let Crowther continue.

'Alex was very unhappy at first,' he began. 'His mother had been ill for some time. It was a long and unpleasant illness, and he took care of her. His father had died some years ago. She and Alex were very close. Anyway, when he came here, he had no family left. We haven't got children of our own, Inspector, and he was like a son to us.'

The age difference between Forley and Mrs Crowther could not be very big. If Forley had left university at the age of twenty-one, like most people, he would now be thirty-seven. Could she really feel like a mother towards a man of that age? Eliot looked at Mrs Crowther, and saw some embarrassment on her face.

'What time were you expecting him this afternoon?' he asked.

'He usually comes about four o'clock.' Her voice changed. 'I can't speak about him in the past tense. I can't believe he'll never come again.'

She put her face in her hands and began to cry quietly.

# Chapter 4
# The sound of a shot

'But Blackheath isn't a violent place, Inspector,' Mr Crowther said. 'We've lived here for thirty years and nothing like this has ever happened before. Of course there's a bit of stealing sometimes, but never murder. We've always felt very safe here.'

Eliot wanted to say that murder could happen anywhere, even in the nicest places. But he only said, 'Hold on, sir. We don't yet know that it was murder.'

'Then you think it looked like suicide?' Mr Crowther asked.

'That's impossible,' his wife said. 'Alex would not have killed himself. What reason could he possibly have had?'

'I don't think anything yet, Mr Crowther,' Eliot replied. 'I just have to consider all the possibilities, including accidental death.'

'Oh, the gun,' Mrs Crowther began. She stopped, and gave her husband a quick look.

There was a silence before Eliot continued.

'Can you tell us about Mr Forley's job?' he asked. 'You said he had a shop in Greenwich.'

'Forley Antiques,' she answered. 'It's one of those big antique furniture shops on Park Street, near the Royal Naval College. You must know it.'

Eliot had been there once, when he was first married, before Sally's birthday. He had seen a small table in the window which he knew she would love. With his recent salary rise, he thought he might be able to afford it. But he had been really shocked to hear the price. The young girl assistant had made him feel quite uncomfortable, and he had left quickly.

'Yes, I've been inside,' he answered. 'But I don't remember seeing Mr Forley.'

'Oh, he doesn't spend much time there,' Mrs Crowther said. 'He doesn't have to. He just chooses the furniture. There's a manager and a part-time assistant who do most of the work.'

She was talking of Forley in the present tense again, as if she could not believe he was dead. She and her husband both looked very tired. Eliot would not get much useful information from them this evening.

'We won't need to stay long,' he said. 'But I'm

afraid we'll have to come back tomorrow. There are just one or two more things I need to know now. Did you notice anything unusual this afternoon?'

The two houses were not attached, and both had thick walls. But it was just possible that the sound of a gunshot next door would be heard here.

'I'm afraid I can't help you, Inspector,' said Mr Crowther. 'I was out most of the afternoon. I went for my usual walk after lunch, and I didn't get back till about ten past four. You didn't hear anything, did you, my dear?' he asked his wife.

She seemed to be choosing her words carefully. 'Well, I do remember hearing a bang while you were out. I was working and I didn't really think about it at the time. I paint pictures, Inspector, and my work takes all my attention. There are so many fireworks at the moment that I didn't give it another thought. But I suppose it is rather unusual to hear a firework in the middle of the afternoon.'

'What time was this?' asked Eliot.

'It must have been after three o'clock,' she said. 'That's when I started painting. Probably around three thirty.'

'Where were you?' he asked.

'In the front room upstairs,' she answered. 'You can see Alex's front door from there. Oh, why didn't I pay more attention? If someone had come out of the house, I could have seen them.'

'Unless they left through the French windows,' Eliot said. 'Now, I'm afraid we'll need someone to identify the body, to be sure it is Mr Forley. You told us he had no relatives when his mother died. Did he ever marry?'

Mrs Crowther covered her face with her hands. Her husband put his arm round her, and answered for her.

'No. He had a girlfriend, though – Amanda Grant. I always thought they would get married some day. We've got her address somewhere. I'll go and get it.'

He came back into the room and handed Eliot the address.

'Please don't contact Miss Grant,' said Eliot. 'We'll give her the news ourselves.'

Eliot nodded at Bowen and they both stood up. They had all the information they were going to get that evening.

# Chapter 5
# New Cross at night

'What I don't understand,' said Bowen when they were in the car again, 'is why a beautiful woman like that would marry someone so much older than herself. What can she see in him?'

Eliot did not answer. During his ten years of marriage, he had often asked himself the same thing about Sally. But he realised the younger man had his own reason for asking the question. What Bowen really wanted to know was why some men were successful with women when he himself was not. Eliot did not know the reason. It was just luck, he supposed, and being attracted to the right kind of woman.

Eliot had seen Bowen's latest girlfriend once or twice, a photographer he had met at a wedding. She was certainly attractive, if you liked tall thin women, but she looked hard. The relationship had been going badly for some time, and she had stopped returning his phone calls. But Bowen was still mad about her. He had been coming to work with dark circles under his eyes recently. And Eliot had twice had to speak to him about being late for work.

'Crowther's obviously crazy about his wife,' Bowen said. 'But how does she feel about him? They couldn't be more different. She's musical and paints. Did you see those wonderful pictures on the wall? But he seems quite ordinary. He must be rich, though, to live in a house like that.'

Eliot let him continue talking. It was more pleasant to think about the Crowthers than the dead man. At least they were alive and still had faces you could recognise. Mrs Crowther seemed to have been especially close to Forley. He would be interested to know what her husband had thought about that. And what had she wanted to say about the gun?

A lot of questions filled his mind. They would all need answers, eventually. But he tried not to guess what these might be. The case had only just begun, and he did not yet know all the facts. It was important to keep his mind as open as possible.

Of course, it might not be a very difficult job. They would probably find that Forley had killed himself. He didn't seem to have left a note, but that wasn't so unusual these days. Eliot hoped they would not have to wait too long for the pathologist's report.

The journey back to New Cross was easier. The traffic was much lighter now, and they were only stopped by one red light. Eliot thought he might even get home in time for the news.

After Blackheath Hill, Bowen had to pay more attention to the road. Driving in many parts of London was like a competition now, with drivers trying to overtake each other as much as possible. And they did not always slow down when they saw a police car.

Suddenly, Bowen had to brake to avoid a crash. A silver-grey Mercedes had been left in the middle of the road with no lights and the engine still running.

'The kids around here!' said Eliot. 'They've got no idea of danger. It's because no-one takes care of them. I suppose stealing cars is the only fun they get, at least until they're old enough to start selling drugs.'

The week before, he had caught two young boys in a stolen car. Their father had been watching football when the police phoned, and he was very angry that he had to go to the police station before the end of the match. The boys were given a strong warning, and then allowed to go. But just two hours later they were back at the police station, with smiles on their faces. After getting home, they had gone straight out to steal another car.

This kind of thing was happening more and more these days, and it worried Eliot. The younger boy had only been ten, just two years older than Micky. What hope was there for a child like that?

Until now, he had managed to protect Micky from the worst elements of city life. But he did not know how much longer this could last. In New Cross, boys had to show they were strong, through fighting or crime. Eliot worried about his gentle son. He and Sally had been talking for a long time about moving to a safer area. He must look at house prices the next time he was in Blackheath.

It took twenty minutes for a policeman to come and take the Mercedes away.

'The owner's going to be pleased to get it back,' said Bowen. 'He's lucky it wasn't stolen by professionals. He'd never have seen it again.'

By now they had passed Goldsmith's College. The pavements were full of young people waiting outside takeaway restaurants or queuing to get into music clubs. The girls looked very cold in thin dresses and jackets. It made Eliot want to turn up the heating in the car. He was lucky Micky was a boy. If he had a daughter, he knew he would worry about her even more.

The police station was quite crowded when he went in to make his report. Friday and Saturday were always the busiest nights. Too much alcohol was drunk by young people, and many had hardly eaten more than a sandwich since breakfast. It was not surprising that they became noisy and violent. There were often fights. 'The English problem,' thought Eliot. 'We're famous for it. We even export it, on holiday and at football matches.'

He bought a takeaway meal from an Indian restaurant and drove home. The news had just finished and he began to watch a comedy programme. He usually enjoyed it but today the jokes didn't seem very funny. Perhaps it was because he was tired. He had had a long day.

Normally, Eliot went to sleep as soon as his head touched the pillow, waking up after exactly eight hours, feeling fresh and lively. But tonight he kept turning from side to side, unable to relax. And when sleep finally came, it gave him no peace.

He dreamed he saw Micky and Sally in the back of

a stolen Mercedes. A gun lay on the seat in front, next to the driver. Eliot watched in fear as the man went faster and faster. He shouted at him to stop. Suddenly the man turned round without slowing the car, and Eliot saw only blood instead of a face. Eliot woke up covered in sweat.

## Chapter 6
# Identifying the body

Eliot woke at 7:45 with the sun on his face. It was strange how things always seemed better in the morning. Last night's worries had completely disappeared, and he was looking forward to the day ahead.

After a quick bath, he went down to get his newspaper from the letter-box. The front page was full of stories of political bribes. He read it with interest while he was having his coffee and toast. It was nice to have a quiet breakfast, for a change. But he wondered what time he could phone Sally. It was too early now. He might wake her parents.

It was surprising how much he wanted to hear her voice. In their ten years of marriage, he had sometimes had to go away for work. He did not mind this occasionally. But she had very rarely left him, and he missed her. He supposed this was why he had slept so badly.

At the police station, Bowen was waiting outside his office.

'Any developments?' asked Eliot.

'Well, sir, we've just heard that there were several people's fingerprints in the house. But on the gun, there were only the dead man's.'

'Not a great help,' said Eliot. 'It could still be suicide. Or an accident. Or murder. Maybe someone shot him, cleaned the gun, and then put it in his hand to look like suicide. Well, we'd better see Amanda Grant and take her to look at the body. Then we'll make another visit to the Crowthers.'

Amanda Grant lived in Greenwich, which was halfway between New Cross and Blackheath. Eliot wanted to start early to avoid the crowds as much as possible.

Thousands of tourists arrived every day from the centre of London. Many were visitors to the Millennium Dome, while others came to see the famous old parts of Greenwich: the Queen's House, the Old Royal Observatory and the *Cutty Sark*, the fastest ship to bring tea from China in the nineteenth century. On Saturdays, the tourists were joined by people from other areas of London. They visited the park and the many markets around the town where you could buy almost anything, old or new.

Bowen had to park the car some distance from where Amanda Grant lived. Her house was not on a road, but looked directly out over the river, with only her garden and a public path in between. It was small, but very attractive.

'It's so quiet, we could almost be in the country,' said Eliot. 'But we're only a few minutes from the centre of Greenwich. I wonder how much this house is worth. Certainly a lot more than I could afford.'

The door was opened by a short, dark-haired woman in her late twenties, dressed in jeans and a long bright-coloured pullover. She looked rather pale and tired. She was not beautiful like Catherine Crowther, but she had an attractive face. Eliot could not remember where he had seen her face before.

'Good morning,' said Eliot. 'I'm Detective Inspector Eliot, and this is Detective Constable Bowen. We'd like to speak to Amanda Grant, if she's at home.'

'I'm Amanda Grant,' she answered. Her voice was unusually deep. 'What can I do for you, Inspector?'

'May we come in, Miss Grant?' asked Eliot. 'It would be easier to talk inside.'

She looked surprised but calmly asked them to come in. The front door opened directly into a sitting room, where bright curtains and carpets gave a warm feeling. A cat was washing itself on a chair. Through the window Eliot could see the yellow and white shapes of the Millennium Dome beside the river. In front of it a boat moved slowly towards the centre of Greenwich. Piano music was coming from a CD player next to a large desk covered with papers and books. At one end a single rose stood in a glass vase. Eliot felt very unwilling to bring the subject of death and guns into this peaceful room.

She did not say a word while he spoke, or for a long time afterwards.

'I suppose you'll want me to identify the body,' she said eventually. 'You obviously need to make sure it's Alex.' Her face showed no sign of what she was feeling.

Eliot wondered how many more strong and intelligent women they would find in Forley's life.

'Yes, I'm afraid so, Miss Grant,' he said. 'We'll take you there now, if you don't mind. After that, we'll need to ask you some questions.'

Her face was pale as she switched off the music and put on her coat. But she was quite calm as she got into the car. Could she really be as cool as she seemed?

Eliot looked at her closely as they went into the building. She still showed no sign of strong feeling. Her hands started to shake only when the body was brought out and the plastic sheet taken off. Of course, the head remained covered. If she could not be sure without seeing the face, they would have to use fingerprints and dentist's records. But he didn't think this would be necessary. Anyone who knew this man would recognise those long fingers. She looked quickly at the body, and nodded at Eliot.

'You're certain?' he had to ask.

She touched the man's right hand for a moment. Then she started to cry.

No-one spoke as they drove back into Greenwich. Unusually for November, the sun was still bright, and many people were carrying their jackets over their arms.

A grey sky would have been more suitable, Eliot thought. It would have matched the sadness in Amanda Grant's eyes. She was staring straight ahead of her. She obviously did not notice the weather or Eliot's face as he turned round to look at her.

# Chapter 7
# Not an easy relationship

The cat jumped off the chair as they entered Amanda Grant's house. It went out of the room, and Bowen followed to look for the kitchen. Since joining the police he had become used to making tea in strange houses. He found most people felt better after a cup if it was strong and very sweet.

Amanda Grant took the drink and thanked him quietly. She tasted it and made a face because of the sugar, but drank it without saying anything.

She seemed quite calm again when Eliot started asking questions.

'I'm a journalist, Inspector,' she said. 'I work for a magazine called *Women in the World*. I don't suppose you've heard of it.'

But he had. Sally had started getting it, and he had looked at it occasionally, trying to understand why it interested her. Suddenly, he remembered where he had seen Amanda Grant's face. It was in the magazine every month, on the inside front page. He had noticed it because it was so much younger than the three other faces there. Obviously, she was a very successful woman.

'I'm afraid I don't have time for magazines, Miss Grant,' he answered, not completely truthfully. 'Have you known Mr Forley long?'

'Almost four years,' she said. 'We met on December 31st, at a New Year's Eve party. After that we started seeing each other quite often.'

'How often?' asked Eliot.

'Oh, several times a week,' she answered. 'But not so much recently.' She turned her face away. 'My new job takes so much of my time that he wanted me to give it up. We had lots of arguments about it. We had one the last time I saw him.'

She put her hand over her eyes.

'And when was that, Miss Grant?' Eliot asked.

'Sunday evening,' she said. 'Then I was away in Edinburgh till yesterday afternoon. I should have phoned during the week, but I was angry with him. I suppose he felt the same. I called yesterday when I got back, but he wasn't in.' Her voice seemed to change a little. 'It was Friday,' she said, 'so I supposed he'd gone to see Catherine Crowther earlier than usual.'

'But I understood he went to see both the Crowthers,' said Eliot, a little more sharply than he had intended.

'That's what Ronald Crowther likes to think,' she answered. 'He was very kind to Alex after his mother died. Alex was alone in the world and he needed Ronald's help at first. But then he got better, and his life changed. He needed Ronald less, but Ronald started to depend on him. Ronald's rather lonely. He doesn't have many friends.'

Eliot looked interested, but said nothing.

'Alex began to find Ronald rather boring,' she continued, 'though he never showed it. He hated hurting people, and he couldn't forget how kind Ronald had been to him. But Alex shared more interests with Catherine. They liked each other a lot, though Ronald never seemed jealous. Ronald's interested in sport, and Alex wasn't. But he used to pretend he was, to make the old man happy.'

'And were you jealous, Miss Grant?' Eliot wanted to ask. But this was not the right time for this question. Instead he looked thoughtfully at a photograph on her desk. It showed a tall thin man with blond hair and dark eyes which were laughing at the camera. A very handsome man. If this was Alex, it was not surprising that he was loved by women.

She followed his eyes, and nodded for the second time that day.

'Yes, that's Alex,' she said.

'Do you mind if we borrow the picture?' asked Eliot.

She gave it to him without a word.

'Is there anything more you'd like to tell us about Mr Forley?' Eliot asked. 'Anything unusual or different?'

'Well, recently he said he'd been feeling weak, and then he started getting headaches,' she replied. 'Before that, he'd never really been ill. He didn't even have a doctor until this year. I suppose that was why he got so worried about his headaches. And he had a lot of time to think about his health. Alex had a lot of money, Inspector, and he hardly needed to work. He could afford to be lazy. Some people might call that lucky, but I wouldn't be happy with a life like that.'

She looked impatient for a moment. Then she continued, 'Anyway, for some reason he got the idea that there was something seriously wrong with his health. But he wouldn't say what he thought it was. He even had some hospital tests a few weeks ago.'

'And what did they show?' asked Eliot.

'I don't know,' she answered. 'The results still hadn't arrived the last time I saw him. I kept telling him that was a good sign. If they had found anything serious, they would have told him immediately.'

'You have to wait for everything these days,' said Eliot, thinking of the pathologist's report. 'Fewer and fewer people do more and more of the work. Well, we'll need his doctor's name and address. Do you know it?'

'Philip Wilver,' she said. 'Alex had known him for years. He works in Blackheath, so when Alex needed a doctor, he was the obvious choice. He lives at 54 Pepys Road, in New Cross.'

'That's a long way from his work,' said Eliot, thinking of last night's traffic jam.

'He couldn't afford a house in Blackheath. He hasn't been a doctor for very long. His family were poor, like mine. We've both had to fight for what we've got. Unlike Alex.'

She looked at the place on the desk where Forley's photograph had been. Then she looked down. Eliot wished he could give it back to her.

'Miss Grant,' Eliot said gently, 'can you think of any reason why Mr Forley might have wanted to kill himself?'

Her face lost all its colour. She looked at Eliot helplessly, and shook her head.

'Would you like us to phone a friend for you?' Eliot asked. 'They could come and sit with you. We'll wait until they arrive.'

'Thank you, Inspector,' she said. 'But I'll be all right alone.'

Eliot and Bowen said goodbye, but she didn't seem to hear them. Eliot wondered if she knew she still had her coat on.

# Chapter 8
# The Blackheath bonfire

The two men were silent for a long time, affected by Amanda Grant's sadness. Eliot had forgotten about Guy Fawkes Night until they got to the top of Blackheath Hill. No children were playing on the grass today. Instead it had a fence around it, with signs telling people to stay out. Inside the fence, there was a lot of activity.

Groups of people were studying pieces of paper and shouting instructions. Workmen were carrying fireworks of all shapes and sizes and piling them onto plastic sheets lying on the ground. In the middle, four men were building a large bonfire.

'I suppose we're lucky Forley died yesterday, and not today,' Eliot said at last. 'The traffic will be worse than ever tonight.'

'What did you think of her, sir?' Bowen asked. 'At first she seemed so cool, like one of those hard career women.'

'I liked her,' said Eliot. 'She doesn't show her feelings easily, but that doesn't mean she doesn't have any. I think she had strong feelings for Forley, though there were obviously problems with their relationship.'

'She didn't say much about Catherine Crowther, did she?' said Bowen. 'I'd love to know what the two women really feel about each other.'

Forley's house looked even more lovely in daylight. Its size and shape were perfect, and the sunlight gave an extra richness to the colour of its old walls. Although it was November, the roses were still beautiful. It seemed impossible that something terrible had happened here the day before.

The telephone was on an antique table next to the wooden stairs in the hall. There were three messages on the answerphone, two from the day before. Amanda Grant had called at 3:45 saying she was back. A few minutes later someone called Philip had invited Forley and Amanda to Sunday lunch. Then at eight o'clock that morning Amanda Grant had phoned again.

'Philip was the name of that doctor Amanda Grant told us about,' remembered Eliot. 'I wonder if it's the same person.'

It was almost half past one when Bowen and Eliot

finished searching the house. Forley had obviously been a very tidy man, and everything seemed to be still in its place. They took away a diary, an address book and £2,200 in cash, which was sitting on top of his desk.

'No-one tried to steal his money,' said Bowen. 'So that's not why he was killed. How can people keep so much cash at home? It's just an invitation to criminals.'

'Oh, he probably thought Blackheath was safe,' Eliot answered. 'Remember what Crowther said? People like that don't believe crime will ever happen to them. We'd better go and see them now. I want to know more about that gun she mentioned.'

But the Crowthers were not at home, so Eliot and Bowen decided to have lunch in an old pub on the edge of Blackheath. Through the window they could see the workmen preparing the evening's firework show.

The bonfire was much bigger now. Groups of people stood looking at the model of Guy Fawkes lying next to it. To Eliot it seemed almost alive with its black hair and beard and seventeenth century hat and coat.

Tonight, many people would watch it burning on top of the bonfire. But few would think about the real Guy Fawkes, who was burned for trying to blow up the Houses of Parliament. His reason had been religious. But most of the people watching tonight would have very little interest in religion. Was anything so important these days that people would kill to protect it? Eliot saw Micky's and Sally's faces in his mind's eye.

He remembered he had to ring them, but the only phone was in the noisiest part of the bar. He sighed. The call would have to wait, but he would look at house prices straight after lunch.

## Chapter 9
# Secrets and lies

Bowen had to ring the bell twice before Catherine Crowther opened the door. Eliot was surprised once again by how lovely she was. She was wearing a green pullover that matched her eyes. And her beauty was strengthened by the unhappiness that showed in her face.

Ronald Crowther was in the sitting room reading a newspaper. He looked up when they walked in, but not before Eliot noticed that his eyes were staring at the top of the front page. He had obviously just picked it up.

He seemed angry and his wife looked very nervous, though they both tried to hide it. They had probably been arguing before the doorbell rang. Eliot decided to question them in different rooms. It would be interesting to see if their stories were the same.

'We'd like to ask you both a few more questions,' he said. 'Mrs Crowther, could you show me where you were painting yesterday? Detective Constable Bowen will speak to Mr Crowther down here.'

He knew that Bowen would have preferred to speak to Catherine Crowther, but the younger man did not let any disappointment show on his face. He got out his notebook as Catherine Crowther led Eliot away.

She took him upstairs to a room with white walls and no furniture, which smelled pleasantly of paint. Eliot could see the backs of several paintings standing against the walls, and another by the window which was not quite finished. The colours were surprising. Unlike the blues and greens of the pictures downstairs, this painting was in black, dark red and orange. It contained a lot of violence. Eliot could hardly believe it had been painted by the same person.

'What made her change to this style of painting?' he wondered. 'And when did it happen? I'd love to know what the paintings over there are like.'

He looked through the window, and had a perfect view of PC Drewitt standing outside Forley's front door with a cigarette in his hand.

If Catherine Crowther spent a lot of time painting up here, she would know all about Forley's private life.

'How long were you up here yesterday?' he asked.

'Most of the morning,' she said. 'I suppose I started painting at about half past nine. I stopped at about twelve o'clock, and began again just after three, as I told you yesterday. But I didn't see any visitors in the afternoon.'

'What about the morning?' asked Eliot.

'Well, someone did come just before I stopped,' she said. 'But I didn't see his face. I only looked up as he was going through the front door.'

'So you have no idea who he was?' Eliot asked.

'Well.' She stopped for a moment. 'From behind he looked a bit like Philip Wilver. He's a friend of Alex's, and his doctor. The man had the same colour hair, and a navy-blue jacket like Philip. But I can't be sure it was him, Inspector. I only saw him for a second.'

'That's very helpful,' said Eliot. 'Do you think your husband saw him?'

'Ronald was working in the back garden all morning,' she said. 'He wouldn't have seen anything. I suppose he might have heard something if they'd gone out into Alex's garden, though. You'd better ask him.'

'We will,' replied Eliot. 'Now, we need to know more about Mr Forley. What kind of man was he?'

She looked into the distance and her eyes filled with tears.

'A very interesting man,' she said. 'And a very kind

one. Sometimes too kind. He hated hurting people, and it made him rather weak.'

She seemed to be sorry she had said this, and went on very quickly, 'It's impossible to believe that anyone would want to hurt him.'

'You said yesterday that you didn't believe it was suicide,' said Eliot. 'What made you so sure?'

She looked away quickly. 'I didn't know what I was saying yesterday, Inspector. Of course, it's possible that he killed himself. Anyone could commit suicide if the situation was difficult enough.'

'And was Mr Forley in a difficult situation?' asked Eliot with interest. Until now he had believed that Alex's life had been easy. Too easy, if Amanda was right.

'Well, I could see he had something on his mind that he wouldn't talk about,' she said. 'But he usually told me everything. He didn't keep secrets.'

'She's talking about him like a lover,' thought Eliot.

'Don't misunderstand me, Inspector,' she said quickly. 'Alex and I were very close. He was probably my best friend, but we didn't have a love affair. My husband had no worries about our relationship. He knew everything that happened between us.'

'I see,' said Eliot, not believing this at all. 'Now, you mentioned a gun last night. Can you tell me more about it?'

'Did I?' she said, looking away. 'I was so shocked yesterday. I've forgotten what I said. But I do remember Ronald and Alex joking about one recently. It was after Alex had bought a valuable painting for his house. Ronald asked if he had ever thought about being robbed, and Alex said he'd better go out and buy a gun. Maybe that's what I was thinking about last night. But neither of them were serious, Inspector. Nothing ever happens in Blackheath.'

She looked as if she knew Eliot did not believe her. She was not a very good liar.

'Now, I understand Mr Forley had been worried about his health,' he went on. 'Could you tell me about it?'

'Oh, yes,' she said quickly, as if pleased to change the subject. 'He'd had a lot of headaches, and he took them very seriously. That was how his mother's illness started, Inspector. She died of a brain tumour, you see, and it wasn't pleasant. Alex was getting really worried.'

'And would you say that Mr Forley was a lazy man?' asked Eliot, remembering what Amanda Grant had said.

'Not at all, Inspector,' she answered. 'He didn't spend all his time doing business, if that's what you mean. But there are many other kinds of work. Alex loved music and books and paintings, and he gave a lot of time to them. Of course, some people would not consider that work, because it doesn't make any money.'

She looked at Eliot as if she was wondering whether he belonged to this group of people.

'What was his relationship with Miss Grant like?' he asked. 'Do you think they were happy together?'

She was quiet for a moment. Then she said, 'Amanda is a young woman of the world, Inspector. She wants to be successful and she couldn't see that Alex's values were different. She didn't always understand him. It caused problems between them.'

'What kind of problems?' asked Eliot.

'Alex wanted to marry her, but she couldn't make up her mind. She wanted him to take more interest in his business. It made Alex very unhappy.'

She looked at Eliot sadly for a moment.

'She didn't realise how lucky she was,' she said. 'And now it's too late. Too late to change anything.'

She put her hand over her eyes to hide her tears.

# Chapter 10
# Falling in love again

Unlike many men, Eliot did not feel uncomfortable when women cried. In his job he was quite used to it. He watched Mrs Crowther closely, but without appearing to. She was clearly unhappy, but it was also obvious that she was hiding something. Maybe it had nothing to do with Forley's death. And maybe Forley's death was suicide. But still he wanted to know what it was.

For the moment, though, he could ask only routine questions.

'There's one more thing that interests me,' he said. 'We've found a lot of money in Mr Forley's house. Did he always keep large amounts of cash at home?'

'I have no idea, Inspector,' she said in surprise. 'Money isn't something I usually discuss.'

'No,' thought Eliot. 'I suppose you don't need to when you've got so much.'

They went out of the door. Eliot stopped in front

of a painting outside the room. It was similar to the ones downstairs.

'May I ask if this is one of yours?' he said.

She nodded, looking surprised again, and he went on, 'It's very different from the one you're working on now.'

'Oh, I wanted to try something new,' she said lightly. She turned quickly towards the stairs, but not before Eliot had seen her face was starting to burn.

Bowen and Ronald Crowther were waiting for them in the hall.

'If there's anything more we can tell you, please ask,' said Ronald Crowther. 'Alex was a wonderful man. We want to do everything we can to help.'

'Oh, there is one thing. I understand you were working outside yesterday morning, sir,' said Eliot. 'Did you hear anything from Forley's garden?'

'Not a thing, I'm afraid, Inspector,' said Ronald Crowther.

He opened the door to let them out, and stood looking at them as they walked down the path towards the gate.

In the car they compared the Crowthers' stories, which seemed to agree in every detail.

'What about that story of the gun, sir?' asked Bowen. 'Do you believe it?'

'Not a word of it,' Eliot said. 'They're obviously lying. I wonder why. What did you think of Ronald Crowther?'

'Well, he's not as intelligent as his wife,' answered Bowen. 'And he's obviously unhappy about Forley, but not as unhappy as she is. I'd say he's worried about something, frightened maybe.'

'I think it would take a lot to frighten a man like Crowther,' said Eliot. 'He doesn't seem to be a man of very much imagination.'

'From what you've said, sir, Catherine Crowther didn't have a very high opinion of Amanda Grant.'

'No, she seemed to feel she understood Forley better than Amanda.'

'Do you think Forley and Catherine Crowther were having an affair, sir?'

'I don't know,' Eliot said. 'She was obviously very close to him because he told her why he was so worried about his headaches. Even Amanda didn't seem to know that.'

'So what's our next move?' asked Bowen.

'Well, we can't question them again before

we've seen the pathologist's report on Monday,' said Eliot. 'But we'll go and see Philip Wilver first thing tomorrow. I wonder if he was the man that Catherine Crowther saw yesterday. His name keeps appearing everywhere. He may have something to tell us.'

They decided to call in at Forley's shop in Greenwich, and as they turned into Park Street they saw streams of tourists walking towards the river. Many were eating ice creams, although it was now quite cold and already starting to get dark.

It was a long street of tall smart houses. Their windows and doors were all the same dark blue, but plants grew everywhere, in front gardens and window boxes, giving it colour and life. There were only two shops, which both sold antiques. They stood side by side, as if they needed each other's company among the houses all around. Above the door of the larger one was Forley's name in gold letters.

The windows held almost nothing. In one there was a small table with a beautiful metal lamp on it. In the other a large Chinese pot stood on a richly coloured Persian carpet.

Eliot must have been mad to imagine he could afford anything here. And the house prices he had seen had amazed him. But he would find the money sooner or later, even if he had to work every weekend for a year.

Although it was only four o'clock, a sign on the door said 'Closed'. But a young woman was sitting at a table inside. He knocked once on the door, and then again, more loudly, when she did not move. He held up his policeman's card, and she came quickly to the door. It was obvious she had been crying.

'I'm Linda Scott,' she said. 'I'm the manager here. I suppose you've come about poor Alex. He was such a lovely man. Of course, I closed the shop immediately when Amanda phoned. Do you have any idea how it happened?'

Eliot was glad she already knew. He did not like giving bad news. He had already had to tell enough people about Forley's death.

'I'm afraid it's still too early to say,' he said. 'But you might be able to help us. Did you see Mr Forley yesterday?'

'Yes. He always came on Fridays,' she said. 'He was here from about nine-thirty to eleven.'

'And did he do anything unusual?' asked Bowen.

'No, I don't think so,' she said. 'He made a few

phone calls and wrote some letters. He did take quite a lot of money away but that wasn't unusual. He said he was planning to buy something. In this business people often prefer to be paid in cash. It stops them having to pay tax.'

She stopped and looked worried. She suddenly seemed to remember she was talking to a policeman.

Bowen smiled at her, though he didn't usually find it funny when people talked about breaking the law.

'Do you know how much money he took?' asked Bowen, still smiling.

'Just over £2,000, I think,' she said, opening a large notebook. 'Yes, £2,200.'

'Just one more thing before we go,' said Eliot. 'Was Mr Forley a good employer?'

'Wonderful,' she said. 'He was kind and human. So different from most employers these days. But recently he'd been looking unhappy. He seemed worried about something. He said he'd been getting headaches, but it must have been more than that.'

Bowen wrote down her address before they left the shop.

'Why was Forley so attractive to women?' he asked Eliot in the car. 'None of them have a bad word to say about him. She seems to have been half in love with him herself.'

'But it didn't do him much good, did it?' said Eliot. 'What's the matter, Bowen? Are you getting jealous of him?'

He had been joking. But a look at Bowen's face showed him the other man was quite serious.

'Just don't get any ideas about Linda Scott until the case is over,' Eliot warned.

'No, sir,' said Bowen.

'You'll have to keep an open mind about her,' continued Eliot. 'She may be guilty of his murder.'

He had no real reason for thinking this. And he had to admit that she seemed nicer than the girls Bowen usually liked. But with Bowen's luck, nothing would surprise him.

## Chapter 11
# Homes and families

At last he was home. Eliot took off his tie, poured himself a beer and rang Sally's parents' number. He half expected no-one to be at home, but Sally picked up the phone before the second ring. She sounded pleased to hear his voice.

'Hello, Rod,' she said. 'Where have you been all day? I rang the station four times.'

'Blackheath and Greenwich mostly,' he replied. 'I've got a new murder, but I'm not getting very far with it. There's a dead man who everybody loved. And a lot of money in his house, but none of it stolen. It might have been suicide, but we won't know till Monday. Are you all right?'

'Yes, we've had a lovely day,' she said. 'It's a pity you had to stay in London. But you sound happier than you were on Friday.'

'Yes, I'm sorry I was in such a terrible mood,' Eliot said. 'How's Micky?'

'Having a great time. But he's missing you a lot. He can't stop talking about you. You'd better have a word with him.'

'Hello, Dad,' said Micky.

Eliot smiled as his son talked about the beach and tonight's firework show. He always got so much pleasure from life. Eliot was sorry not to be with him.

But when he put the phone down, he realised he felt tired. The thought of a quiet evening in front of the television suddenly seemed very pleasant. *Match of the Day* would be enough excitement for this evening, if he could keep awake long enough to watch it.

He was pleased that Sally was not angry with him. In fact, she was never angry for long. But it did not stop Eliot feeling uncomfortable after arguments. There could always be a first time.

He made himself some food, went into the sitting room and turned on the news. The government was in trouble again. Eliot tried to listen to the details through the sounds of fireworks exploding outside. But he was too tired to be very interested.

He fell asleep in the middle of the Saturday night hospital drama. But the shouting of football fans woke him up after two hours. West Ham had just scored the winning goal, three minutes from the end. Eliot smiled as he turned off the television.

Next morning the weather had changed. It was the first day of winter.

When he arrived at the office, Bowen was already there. Eliot thought he had not looked so happy for months.

'Morning, Bowen. Did you have a good evening?' he asked.

'Well, I thought Forley's diary might help us, sir,' he said. 'So I took it home to look at. He obviously didn't want anyone else to understand it. It's written in Greek and Latin mixed together, but I think I'm just beginning to see how it works. It will take a bit of time, though, before I can read it.'

'Education is a wonderful thing,' said Eliot. But he himself had joined the police as soon as he left school. And he did not think a university education would have helped him very much. Reading had never been important to him. He preferred learning from experience.

But he was pleased with the younger man. Bowen was always a fast worker, and now he had an extra interest in the case. The sooner they finished it, the sooner he could try his luck with Linda Scott. Eliot hoped his feelings for her would not affect his judgement.

'Well, we'd better go and see Philip Wilver,' said Eliot. 'Let's hope he's at home.'

'Most people are on Sunday morning,' said Bowen. 'Except policemen.'

Pepys Road was a beautiful street very near Eliot's own house. The houses were large, with big rooms and high ceilings. Many had been separated into flats, but Number 54 was still a single house. Eliot had sometimes looked in through the lighted windows on winter evenings. It always looked inviting with its beautiful fireplace and the large mirror on the wall above it.

Eliot was sad to see the roses in the front garden were turning brown, probably because of last night's cold weather, he thought. They would soon be dead. He knew he would find the same in his own garden, when he had time to look.

Bowen rang the doorbell while Eliot looked through the window, blowing on his hands to keep them warm. A man and a young boy were sitting together on a sofa. They were looking at a picture book. Eliot was disappointed to see that no-one had lit the fire.

The door was opened by a tall dark-haired woman with a cigarette in her hand. She looked pale and stressed. She stared at them for a few seconds without speaking. It was as if she didn't see them.

'Yes?' she said eventually.

'We'd like to speak to Philip Wilver,' said Eliot after he had introduced them. 'Is he at home?'

She went inside and called, 'Philip! It's the police.'

A few seconds later, the man from the sofa appeared. He was tall and good-looking with short dark hair and glasses. He looked nervous, like his wife, but seemed more in control. The young boy was with him, holding on to his leg and staring at the policemen with wide eyes. Eliot thought he must be about five years old.

'I'm Philip Wilver,' said the man. 'I'm sorry my wife kept you waiting outside. Please come in.'

They went into the room Eliot had seen from the outside. It was surprisingly untidy. Papers and magazines lay on the floor next to unwashed cups and ashtrays full of cigarette ends. But this did not hide the fact that it was a beautiful room.

'I'm sorry about the mess,' said Wilver. 'Some friends came over yesterday morning and gave us some terrible news. A friend of ours has died suddenly.'

He looked at them sadly.

'I suppose that's why you've come,' he said.

'I'm afraid so, sir,' said Eliot.

Wilver put his hand on the boy's shoulder.

'Go and find your mother, Sam,' he said. 'She's in the back room.'

The child got up slowly and went out. He did not say a word.

'He's very unhappy about Alex,' said his father. 'Alex was very good with kids. Sam really loved him. Have you found out what happened to him, Inspector?'

'Not yet, sir,' said Eliot. 'But we're hoping you may be able to help us. We understand you knew him quite well. You were also his doctor, weren't you?'

'Only for a few months, Inspector,' said Wilver. 'I knew him better as a friend.'

'We've heard he was ill,' said Eliot. 'Is this true?'

'Not really,' replied Wilver. 'Though for a time he thought he was. He'd been having a lot of headaches and thought they might be serious. But I knew they weren't. He even persuaded me to arrange some tests at Guy's Hospital. A complete waste of money. But that was all I could do to stop him worrying.'

'When are you expecting the results?' asked Eliot.

'Oh, they arrived this week. Of course they showed nothing. He probably just needed a new pair of glasses.'

He turned away again. 'Poor Alex,' he said.

## Chapter 12
# One kind of marriage

No-one spoke for a few seconds. From the next room they could hear Wilver's wife talking to the child. She sounded angry. The boy did not seem to be saying anything.

'Excuse me, Inspector,' said Wilver. 'I'd better get Sam. Lisa's finding him rather difficult at the moment. She's been badly affected by Alex's death. We all have.'

He went out for a moment, and reappeared carrying his son. The boy was crying, his head pressed against his father's shoulder.

'It's all right, Sam,' said Wilver gently. 'Mummy's just a bit busy at the moment.'

'She's always busy,' Sam said. 'She never plays with me.'

'I'll take you to the park soon,' said his father. 'We'll have a game of football. But I must speak to these people first. Go upstairs and get ready, Sam. I think I saw the football in your bedroom this morning.'

The boy stopped crying and went to the door.

'We'll be as quick as we can, sir,' said Eliot. 'Now, how long had you known Mr Forley?'

'Since university,' said Wilver. 'We met on our first day and found we had a lot in common. Both of us had a parent who died when we were very young. It seemed to bring us together. And when I met Lisa, she liked him, too. That was very important. Are you married, Inspector?'

Eliot said he was.

'So you'll understand what it's like,' Wilver continued. 'Alex came from a rich family, like Lisa, and that was important to her. She didn't seem to like my other friends, and eventually I stopped seeing them. Lisa was very unhappy when I started my medical studies. I had to work very hard, and she didn't see much of me. I couldn't expect her to spend time with people she didn't like. You know how it is, Inspector.'

'Of course,' said Eliot. But really he did not understand that kind of relationship. Sally and he had always accepted each other's friends.

'And when did you last see Mr Forley?' he asked.

'Friday,' said Wilver. 'When I phoned to give him his test results, he asked me to come round the next day. He said he wanted my advice about something. So I went to his house at about twelve o'clock. But when I got there, he'd changed his mind. He said it wasn't important any more, though he seemed a bit worried about something. I only stayed for a quick cup of coffee. Then I went back to the surgery for my lunchtime meeting.'

'Do you remember what time you left, sir?' asked Bowen.

'Around twenty past twelve,' said Wilver. 'But I couldn't help worrying about him after that. I phoned later to ask him to lunch today, but he wasn't there. I left a message on his answerphone. I expect you've heard it.'

His face changed.

'Was he already dead by then, Inspector?' he asked.

'I'm afraid we don't yet know,' Eliot replied. 'Dr Wilver, was Mr Forley drinking wine when you were there?'

'Wine?' asked Wilver. 'No. Alex didn't drink very much. And he certainly never drank by himself.'

'Thank you, sir,' said Eliot. 'Now, there's just one more thing I'd like to ask. What kind of person was Mr Forley?'

Wilver looked at him for a moment.

'It's difficult to describe someone you know well,' he said. 'But I'll try. He was easy to talk to. You could tell him anything, and he'd always say the right thing. He was often serious, but he could be very funny, too. I'm going to miss him a lot.'

'And would you say he was a weak man, sir?' asked Eliot, remembering what Catherine Crowther had said.

The doctor did not answer immediately. He looked at the fireplace and seemed deep in thought for a moment.

'No more than the rest of us, Inspector,' he said at last.

He suddenly made himself smile as Sam came into the room, holding a football. The boy looked at Eliot and sat down on the carpet.

Just before they left, Eliot asked, 'By the way, sir. Can you think of anyone who might have wanted to hurt Mr Forley?'

'No,' said Wilver. 'Everyone loved Alex.'

He closed the front door. Through the window, Eliot saw Sam sitting on the floor, patiently waiting for his father. He could not remember Micky ever sitting so still at that age. For a moment he felt worried about the child. What kind of family life did he have?

'What did you think of him?' asked Eliot as soon as they were in the car.

'Well, he obviously loves his son,' said Bowen. 'But I wouldn't like to be in his shoes. Not with a wife like that. She's good-looking enough, but she obviously rules his life. And she doesn't seem to have much time for the kid.'

'But he must be stronger than he looks,' Eliot said. 'His wife couldn't stop him becoming a doctor. And it can't be easy being married while you're training. Of course, you can see why she wouldn't like it. Not just for the long hours. She's too interested in money, and new doctors don't earn very much.'

He looked at Bowen for a moment.

'This should be a lesson for you,' he said. 'Be careful with the women you choose. And if they don't make you happy, get rid of them.'

Bowen looked embarrassed, and Eliot changed the subject.

'Forley was certainly popular,' he said. 'And not only with women. But I'd love to know what Wilver was thinking about when I asked if he was weak.'

'Yes,' said Bowen. 'He's hiding something from us,

too.'

'Well, at least we now know it was Wilver who visited Forley on Friday,' said Eliot. 'And we know that Forley wasn't really ill. That takes away one possible reason for suicide. So what else was he worried about?'

'And why was he drinking if he never drank alone?' Bowen asked. 'Maybe someone came to see him after Wilver had left. Someone who was going to sell him something, perhaps. That could be why he had all that money in the house. Maybe that person murdered him, and then washed the second wine glass.'

'It's possible,' said Eliot. 'But who wanted to murder him? Everyone seemed to like him so much. We'll have to talk to the neighbours again and see if anyone saw anything. Can you arrange that? And you'd better take Amanda Grant to look at his house. It didn't look as if anything was missing, but we ought to be sure. I've got a feeling that this case isn't going to be as easy as I first thought.'

## Chapter 13
# Home at last

Eliot sat at his computer and looked at a report he had started on Friday. But questions about the Forley case filled his mind, and he couldn't push them away.

Why were the Crowthers not telling him the truth? Had Catherine Crowther been having an affair with Forley? What had made her suddenly change her style of painting? And did anyone visit Forley after Wilver had left on Friday? Catherine Crowther would not have seen if they had arrived after one o'clock and gone out through the back gate. And what had Forley been so worried about?

Eliot made a great effort to work. He had three other reports to write, and they should all have been finished days ago. But he couldn't stop thinking about the case. By the time he went home, he had hardly written anything.

'Dad!' said Micky as soon as he got through the door. 'Did you see that brilliant goal last night?'

'On *Match of the Day*?' Eliot asked. 'Weren't you in bed by then?'

'Mum said I could stay up and watch it,' Micky said.

'He could hardly keep his eyes open,' said Sally.

'Neither could I,' said Eliot. He gave them both a kiss.

Sally had already started the evening meal. Eliot rarely cooked, except for Sunday lunch and on Wednesdays when Sally worked late. She taught part-time at Lewisham College. Her classes were usually over in time to pick up Micky from school at 3:30, and on other days her sister took care of him.

As soon as he sat down at the kitchen table, he relaxed. Forley's death was a problem which interested him, but did not worry him any more. Forley had had no children or family of his own. Of course, his friends would miss him, but they had their own lives. And Amanda Grant was strong enough to start again. It was not Eliot's business if the Crowthers and the Wilvers had problems with their marriages. He hoped the pathologist would say it was suicide, and that would be the end of it.

But Eliot's feelings told him it was more complicated than suicide. And after eighteen years with the police, he trusted his feelings. He knew that two people were lying, and maybe more. What were they trying to protect?

Still, it could all wait until tomorrow. Now it was time for him to listen to Micky. He smiled as his son began to tell him about last night's firework show.

# Chapter 14
# But was it murder?

Eliot usually found Monday mornings especially unpleasant when he had been working all weekend. But today he woke up in a good mood, which continued until he got to the police station.

Once again, Bowen had arrived before him. He said he had already been there for half an hour.

'What's happened to you?' asked Eliot. 'Last week you could hardly get here on time. It must be love.'

Bowen wished Eliot would stop mentioning his private life.

'I'm just interested in the case,' Bowen answered uncomfortably. 'And there'll be a lot to do today. By the way, Amanda Grant couldn't find anything missing from Forley's house.'

'As I expected,' said Eliot. 'Have we got any of the reports yet?'

'Yes, sir. The pathologist's has just arrived,' answered Bowen. 'It seems they start work early there. And we've got a report on the gun. It's an army gun from the Second World War. They're not very common now. It's almost a collector's piece. There's no record of it anywhere, of course.'

'That's a pity,' said Eliot. 'There won't be much chance of finding where it came from. It's probably been hiding in someone's garage for years.'

Eliot got a cup of coffee from the machine, and sat down to read the pathologist's report.

'Let's hope this tells us something more useful,' he said. 'Did he kill himself or not? That's what we need to know.'

But his hopes were disappointed. The report said that the dead man had been killed by a shot to the head, fired either by himself or another person, between 3:15 and 3:45 in the afternoon. At the time of death, the gun was touching his forehead and he had died immediately. There were no other signs of violence. He had been in very good health, but there was a lot of alcohol in his stomach and blood.

'Well, it doesn't look as if it was an accident,' said Eliot. 'A man would not sit down in a comfortable chair and put a gun to his head unless he meant to kill himself. But who fired the shot? What do you think, Bowen? Was it murder or suicide?'

'Too many people are hiding things from us,' said Bowen. 'I don't believe it was simple suicide. Though someone obviously wanted us to think it was.'

'Is suicide ever simple?' asked Eliot. 'But I think you're right. Now, we know more or less when he died. And the noise that Catherine Crowther heard at half past three was probably the gunshot. That's if she was telling the truth. Find out who's got an alibi for that time, Bowen. And we'll have to get fingerprints. We'll need to see if any of them match the ones we found in Forley's house.'

'Yes, sir,' said Bowen. 'And Forley seems to have drunk quite a lot. Much more than one glass of wine.'

'So maybe you were right, Bowen,' said Eliot. 'Maybe Forley did invite someone to lunch that day. What did the neighbours say?'

'Nothing important. No-one saw anything.'

'Or maybe Forley drank to make it easier to kill himself,' continued Eliot thoughtfully. 'Everyone keeps saying he was worried about something. Have you found anything useful in his diary?'

'Not yet,' said Bowen. 'It's slow work. It's a long time since I read any Latin or Greek. But I'll keep trying.'

Eliot sat down at his desk. Yesterday's work stared up at him. He hoped he would be able to finish all his reports before Bowen got back. He sighed. Detectives had to do a lot of writing these days. The job had not always been like this.

Eliot worked through the lunch hour, and he managed to finish the last report just after half past two. He put his coat on, and went across the road to The Queen's Head. The barman started pouring him a beer as soon as he walked through the door.

The pub was empty now except for a noisy group of students at one end of the bar. They had all finished their drinks but they didn't seem to be in any hurry to leave.

Eliot sat down by the window, as far away as possible. The beer tasted good. He opened his newspaper and turned to the sports page. He decided to give himself half an hour's break. He had certainly earned it after all that writing.

But he had only just started the report on Saturday's West Ham match when Bowen walked through the door. Eliot sighed. But the news Bowen gave him took all thoughts of football from his mind.

# Chapter 15
# Uncovering lies

'Sorry, sir,' said Bowen. 'But I thought you'd want to hear this as soon as possible. It seems that Forley had a cleaning lady, a Mrs Brook. She went to his house this morning, and got angry when they wouldn't let her in. Mondays and Thursdays were the days she worked for him. And she worked for the Crowthers on Wednesdays.

'Anyway, she's given us some very interesting information. It seems that Forley went to see Catherine Crowther on Wednesday afternoon, when Ronald was out.'

'That *is* interesting,' said Eliot. 'Mrs Crowther told us she hadn't seen him for a week. What did Mrs Brook say about the visit?'

'Apparently, Forley was there for about an hour,' Bowen replied. 'The sitting room door was closed, so she couldn't hear anything. But when they came out, Mrs Crowther was as white as a sheet, and Forley looked very uncomfortable.'

'I wonder what Catherine Crowther will have to

say about that,' said Eliot.

'But that's not all, sir,' continued Bowen. 'Mrs Brook said that Crowther had an old gun. Apparently, it had belonged to his father. She came into the room once when he was cleaning it. He quickly put it back into a drawer in his desk, but not before she had seen it. She said she could never go into the sitting room again without wondering if it was still there.'

'He kept it in a desk?' said Eliot. 'That was stupid. And I don't suppose he had a licence for it. Well, that gives us something to think about. What about the fingerprints? Have you had any luck with them?'

'Well, sir,' said Bowen. 'There were four sets of fresh fingerprints found in the house besides Forley's.'

'So, all we have to do is find out whose fingerprints they are. Our suspects are the Crowthers, the Wilvers, Amanda Grant and Mrs Brook. Can we be sure about what any of them were doing on Friday afternoon?'

'Well, we know Mrs Brook spent the day with her sister. And Wilver was in the surgery from twelve forty-five to six o'clock,' said Bowen. 'He had two meetings, and then he saw patients. He didn't have a free moment. And his wife was having lunch with a friend in Greenwich. She left at three-fifteen to pick up her son from school.'

'What about the other three?' asked Eliot.

'We haven't been able to check their stories,' said Bowen. 'Catherine Crowther was alone at home. Ronald was out walking, but he doesn't remember seeing anybody. And Amanda Grant went straight to her house when she got back.

'But there's something else, sir,' he continued. 'I looked at a few more pages of Forley's diary while I was waiting at the surgery, and I found something very interesting. It seems Alex Forley wasn't the golden boy everybody thinks he was. He was having a secret love affair.'

'With Catherine Crowther?' asked Eliot.

'I'm afraid I can't tell you that,' said Bowen. 'He changed everyone's names.'

'Well, I think we'd better go and have a look at Ronald's gun, don't you?' said Eliot.

He stood up, leaving his beer half drunk. The students were still sitting at the other end of the bar. They would probably stay all afternoon if the barman let them. It was much warmer in the pub than in the rooms which they rented.

Eliot felt some excitement as he rang the Crowthers'

bell. The pieces seemed to be coming together. With any luck the case would be over by the evening.

But neither of the Crowthers were at home.

'I suppose he's gone for his usual walk,' said Eliot. 'But I wonder where she can be. I thought she'd be painting in her room.'

He looked up at the window. Was it his imagination, or did he see someone moving quickly away from the window? He rang the bell again, this time for at least five seconds. But again there was no reply.

'Let's wait in that pub where we went on Saturday,' he said. 'At least it's warm in there, and I can have the second half of my lunch.'

Today the pub was much less crowded, and they easily found a seat. Eliot looked outside, and at first forgot that Saturday had been Guy Fawkes Night. There was no fence and there were no fireworks. People were walking about as usual, and the only sign of the bonfire was a dark shape on the ground.

Suddenly, he saw a tall man in a dark coat on the other side of the grass. Eliot thought he recognised him.

'I think that's Ronald Crowther,' he said. 'Don't you, Bowen?'

But the barman, who was bringing Eliot a sandwich, answered instead.

'Yes, that's Mr Crowther, sir,' he said. 'He's always here at this time, in rain or sunshine. He comes at three o'clock and goes at four. Regular as a clock. Most people would find it boring walking up and down the same piece of grass, never talking to anyone. But he doesn't seem to mind. People are strange.'

'I don't suppose you noticed him here on Friday,' said Eliot.

'Friday?' the barman said. 'Of course I did. I see him every day. At first I thought he was late, but it was my watch that was fast. Like I said, you can tell the time from his coming and going.'

As Eliot finished his sandwich, he saw Crowther turn back to his house. He checked his watch. Exactly four o'clock. The barman had been telling the truth. So Crowther had been out for a walk when Forley died.

But the policemen followed him back to his house anyway. Ronald Crowther could not be the murderer, but he and his wife still had a lot of questions to answer.

# Chapter 16
# Jealousy

Eliot did not return the Crowthers' smiles when they opened the door. He knew they were not at all pleased to see him. Their politeness and gentleness were just a cover. They had been playing games with him from the beginning.

Without any introduction, he asked if Crowther had a gun. The man's face went white, and his wife sat down quickly, as if her legs had lost all their strength.

'And I'd like the truth this time,' said Eliot. 'We've wasted enough time already.'

'Yes, Inspector,' said Crowther. 'I've had a gun for years. It belonged to my father. He kept it to remember the war, and he also kept one bullet. When he died, I kept it to remember him. I suppose that was a stupid thing to do.'

'It was a crime if you had no licence for it,' said Eliot. 'May I see it, please?'

Ronald Crowther covered his face with his hands.

'I haven't got it, Inspector. Alex took it about three weeks ago. We were having friends to dinner, and someone started discussing the war. I'd drunk rather a lot, and stupidly told them about it. Alex loved old things, and of course he wanted to see it.

'Then he said it might be worth a lot of money. He asked if he could borrow it to have it valued. I couldn't see any harm in it, so I gave it to him. I told him there was a bullet inside, but he wasn't worried. He said he knew how to use guns. He'd been taught at school.'

Eliot could feel his anger rising inside him. What kind of world did these people think they were living in? Did they think they were above the law?

'And who else was at this dinner party?' asked Eliot.

But he felt he knew the answer before it came. The Crowthers, the Wilvers and Amanda Grant, the tight little circle that had surrounded Forley until he died.

'Why didn't you tell us this before?' he asked.

Ronald Crowther said he wished he had. But then he had suddenly realised that keeping a gun was against the law. He and his wife had decided that the best thing to do was to keep quiet.

'Mr Crowther, we'll have to ask you to come to the police station immediately,' said Eliot. 'We need to know if it was your gun which killed Mr Forley.'

The Crowthers looked at each other. They seemed

frightened.

'And Mrs Crowther, could you tell us when you last saw Mr Forley?' Eliot asked.

She lifted her green eyes to his.

'As I told you, Inspector,' she answered, 'it was a week ago on Friday.'

'Could you think very carefully about that?' said Eliot.

'I don't need to,' she said. 'I remember very well.'

'Mrs Crowther,' said Eliot. 'I'll have to ask you to come to the station with us too. We need to question you again about the death of Alex Forley.'

'*Me*?' she said. 'You want to question *me*? But I thought ...'

She stopped suddenly. Ronald Crowther had closed his eyes. He looked like a man in the middle of a bad dream.

Eliot told Bowen not to leave the couple alone together. He didn't want to give them a chance to think of another story.

At the police station, they were taken to separate rooms. They both nodded when Eliot showed them the gun.

Ronald Crowther was looking tired and much

older than when Eliot had first seen him, and his wife suddenly seemed middle-aged. Eliot decided to question her first.

'We have spoken to someone who says Mr Forley visited you last Wednesday afternoon,' he said.

'Have you? I suppose it was Mrs Brook,' she answered after a short silence. 'I forgot all about her.'

Perhaps people like Mrs Brook were not important enough for her to remember. Eliot wondered again what sort of person Alex Forley had been. How could a man be so close to two such different women as Catherine Crowther and Amanda Grant?

'Yes, it's true,' Catherine Crowther continued. 'Alex did come to see me then. We discussed something very private. Alex even asked me not to tell Ronald about it.'

'Nothing is private after a violent death,' said Eliot impatiently. 'As you should know very well.'

She was silent for a long time.

'Well, Alex had been having a secret relationship,' she said at last. 'I suppose you'd call it an affair, though he was very unhappy about it. It started one evening after a party, when Amanda was away and he was feeling lonely and unhappy. Of course, he immediately wished it hadn't happened. But the woman said she was in love with him, and he didn't know how to end it without hurting her. She was the wife of a friend of his. That's what made it so awful. And that's why I didn't tell you before.'

'Who was she?' asked Eliot.

'Lisa Wilver,' said Catherine Crowther, looking angry.

'Mrs Crowther, were you in love with Mr Forley?' asked Eliot.

She looked at Eliot for a moment.

'Perhaps I was,' she answered. 'We were so close, but nothing ever happened, Inspector. I would never do anything to hurt Ronald. He has been so good to me.'

'And how did you feel when you heard about this affair?'

'Very angry. You've seen my latest painting, Inspector. But it wasn't just jealousy. I thought Alex was so stupid. Lisa's not a very nice person, though he always believed the best of everybody. Her husband's crazy about her, but she doesn't care about him, or her son. She liked Alex because he had money. She thought she had got him, and she wasn't going to let him go. Alex wasn't strong enough to end it. And then, of course, he got so worried about his health.'

'What did you say to him about the affair?' asked Eliot.

'I told him he should finish it immediately,' she answered. 'I also told him how stupid I thought he had been.'

'And why didn't you tell us before about your last meeting with Mr Forley?'

'Oh, I don't really know, Inspector. It was silly of me.'

She really was not a good liar, Eliot thought again. He felt very impatient. What reason could she have for continuing to lie? He knew about the gun, about Alex's last visit and about his affair. And she'd even admitted her own jealousy. What else could she have to hide?

And then Eliot realised. She must be trying to protect her husband.

'Mrs Crowther,' he said, 'we know that your husband was nowhere near Mr Forley's house when he died.'

She stared at Eliot. She seemed unsure about whether to believe him.

'Somebody saw him when he was out walking,' he continued.

'Oh, thank God,' she said. 'I've been so afraid. I

didn't know Ronald could be jealous until recently. But suddenly he started asking questions about my relationship with Alex. He couldn't stop talking about it. Alex hadn't spent much time with him lately because he was too worried about his own problems. But Ronald thought it had something to do with me. I don't know if Ronald was more jealous of Alex or of me, but it was very frightening.

'I didn't really believe he'd killed Alex. But he kept asking if Alex ever came to see me when he was out. I couldn't tell him about Wednesday's visit because Alex had made me promise not to. But I think perhaps Ronald saw him leaving the house. Anyway, Ronald could see I was very unhappy about something.

'I didn't want to make the situation worse by telling you about Alex's visit in front of him. Of course, there was nothing for him to be jealous about. Believe me, Inspector. Nothing ever happened between me and Alex.'

Except, perhaps, in your mind, thought Eliot.

At last, he felt she was telling him the truth. As a strong woman, she was clearly not used to lying. But her guilt about her feelings for Forley had made her very confused. And it had wasted a lot of his time.

He watched Catherine and Ronald Crowther leave the police station together. They had obviously been living in fear for the last few days, each believing the other had killed Forley. He wondered how they would explain this when they got home.

'But if neither of them murdered Alex Forley, how did he die?' thought Eliot. 'At last we know what was worrying him so much recently. But surely his relationship with Lisa Wilver wasn't enough to make him kill himself.

'It's true we've now found two other people who possibly wanted him dead. Philip Wilver, if he knew about his wife's affair. And Lisa Wilver, if Forley had tried to finish it. But both of them were with other people that afternoon. There's no question about that.

'No. If someone had been with Forley on Friday afternoon, there was only one person it could be.'

## Chapter 17
# Putting the pieces together

Amanda Grant looked surprised when she opened the door to Eliot and Bowen. But she calmly asked them to come in. She was wearing the same jeans and sweater as on Saturday morning, and today she seemed more like a teenage girl than a successful journalist.

Eliot felt very disappointed. He had liked her from the moment he had first seen her, and he was not usually so wrong about people. She was certainly a woman of strong character and feelings. And he believed most people could kill if the situation was right. Perhaps she had found out about Forley's affair and been unable to accept it. But he had thought she was a brave person. Why hadn't she admitted the crime immediately, instead of trying to cover it up?

'Miss Grant,' he said, 'we would like to know exactly what you did when you got back from Edinburgh.'

'I told Detective Constable Bowen this morning,' she said, in her deep voice. 'The plane landed at

London City Airport at five past two. I picked up my car from the car park, and drove back. It took over an hour. The traffic was terrible that day.'

'I understand nobody saw you,' continued Eliot.

'No,' she answered. 'Is it important?'

'These are just routine questions,' said Eliot. 'Now, what did you do when you got home?'

'I unpacked and had a bath,' she said. 'Then I tried to phone Alex, as you'll know if you've checked his answerphone.'

'Miss Grant, do you have a mobile phone?' asked Eliot.

'Of course,' she answered. 'But I didn't use it to ring Alex, if that's what you're asking. I used that phone over there.'

Eliot was suddenly very pleased. Her story would be easy to check. The airport car park would be able to tell them when she had left, and the phone company would have a record of her calls. If she had phoned from home, it would not have been possible for her to kill Forley. With all that traffic, she could not have got to his house before 3:20 at the earliest. And she certainly would not have been home again by 3:45. For once, he was thankful for the traffic.

In the car Bowen was silent, and Eliot knew he was angry with himself. He had forgotten to ask her about the mobile phone when he saw her that morning. But it would only have saved a little time. Much less time than they had wasted on the Crowthers.

Back at the station, it took Bowen only twenty minutes to check Amanda's story. Someone from her office in Edinburgh had driven her to the airport, and the plane had arrived at five past two, as she had said. Both the car park and the phone company gave the same information as she had given them.

'So it looks as though she is not guilty either,' said Eliot. 'And she's the one who gets everything he owned. We've just spoken to his lawyer. It seems Forley made a will two weeks ago, and left everything to her. But I'm not sure how pleased she'll be. She didn't seem very comfortable about his money.'

Was this case really as unusual as it seemed? Money or love were at the root of most situations the police had to work with. And there were plenty of both here. He felt they must have something to do with Alex Forley's death. But he could not discover what it was. He was finding more and more people with a reason for killing Forley. But it seemed that none of them had had the opportunity.

Eliot did not believe Lisa Wilver would tell them anything useful when they spoke to her. He was beginning to think that Alex Forley had killed himself after all.

That evening, Eliot was quieter than usual, though he always tried not to bring his work home. It was not fair that his family should suffer because of his job. He made a great effort to listen to one of Micky's long stories about his school friends. But Eliot felt something about the case was wrong. He trusted his feelings, and he didn't have much time.

'So then Paul hit David, and Miss Thomas made him sit by himself for half an hour. I'm glad he hit him,' Micky was saying.

'But you shouldn't hit people,' said Eliot automatically.

'Yes, but do you know what David did, Dad? He told Paul Miss Thomas had given us five pages of homework, but she hadn't given us any.'

'Why did he tell a lie like that?' Eliot tried to be interested.

'Paul broke his pen and he was angry with him. Do you know how long Paul took to do his homework?

Two and a half hours. And he hates maths. Wasn't David horrible? Dad! What are you doing? Put me down!'

Eliot had suddenly picked up his surprised son and was dancing with him round the kitchen.

'Thanks, Micky,' he said. 'I understand it now. Your story was a great help.'

Eliot had suddenly realised what he had missed. Now he thought he knew what had happened to Forley. But before he could be sure, there was something he needed to check. And he would have to ask Bowen to finish reading Forley's diary.

## Chapter 18
# The truth at last

'But why have you brought me here?' asked Dr Wilver. 'I'm a very busy man.'

Eliot had chosen the biggest and smartest of the interview rooms. It had just been painted and the furniture was new. He wanted Wilver to feel relaxed.

'Oh, we just need a little more information,' said Eliot. 'It's completely routine. And we'd like to record this interview. You don't mind, do you, sir?'

Wilver shook his head and Eliot switched on the cassette machine.

'Now, could you tell us again about your last meeting with Mr Forley?' he asked.

Wilver repeated what he had told them the last time they had seen him. At first he seemed nervous, as if he was waiting for Eliot to speak. But he soon began to relax. Eliot listened carefully and nodded from time to time.

'Thank you, sir,' he said politely, after Wilver had finished. 'And now, would you tell us again where you were on the afternoon when he died? This is just routine, of course. We have to ask everybody.'

Wilver relaxed even more.

'Yes, of course, though I did tell Detective Constable Bowen yesterday. I was in the surgery all afternoon. Plenty of people saw me. I'm surprised you haven't asked them, Inspector. But perhaps you've been busy, too.'

He smiled at Eliot. But the smile began to disappear after Eliot's next question.

'Dr Wilver, when did you give Mr Forley his test results?'

'As I told you, I phoned him on Thursday evening. You can check with the phone company.'

'And when did you receive them from the hospital, sir?' asked Eliot.

Dr Wilver looked away.

'Probably on Thursday morning,' he said. 'But it's difficult to remember exactly.'

'Even when the patient is a good friend who is seriously worried about them?' asked Eliot.

'I'm afraid so, Inspector. We get so many test results,' said Wilver.

A line of sweat appeared on his forehead.

'Well, let me help your memory,' he said. 'The hospital phoned to give you the results on Monday

morning. Now, could you tell us why you waited so long to pass them on to Mr Forley?'

The doctor dried his forehead with a handkerchief.

'It just escaped my memory,' he said. 'I was very busy all last week.'

'But not too busy to go and see Mr Forley on Friday. No, I don't believe that. I think you had a very good reason for keeping the results secret, Dr Wilver.'

'What can you possibly mean?' asked the doctor.

'I think you know what I mean,' said Eliot. 'When you phoned Mr Forley on Thursday, I don't think you gave him his test results. I think you told him you needed some money and wanted to sell something. That's why he took so much cash home. Then when you went to see him on Friday, you lied about his results. You told him he had a brain tumour. You knew that he was planning to kill himself if the test showed he had one. He'd discussed it with you. And you knew he had Crowther's gun.'

'I don't know what you're talking about,' said Wilver. 'Alex never discussed killing himself with me. If he had, I would have told him not to. I'm a doctor, and I was his friend. What reason would I have had? You've been watching too much television, Inspector.'

'The reason was your wife, Lisa,' said Eliot. 'You knew she was having an affair with Mr Forley. And you knew she wanted to leave you for him. You couldn't allow that, could you, sir? We have Mr Forley's diary. We know all about the affair, and we know he told you about his plans to kill himself.'

At the mention of the diary, all the blood seemed to leave Wilver's face. He put his head in his hands. There was a long silence. When he started to speak, Eliot and Bowen had to move forward to hear what he was saying.

'Alex never had to fight for anything,' he said. 'He had everything he wanted. But he couldn't take Lisa away. I wouldn't let Sam grow up without a mother, as I had to. I've worked so hard for what I've got. I wouldn't let anyone take it away from me. You were right, Inspector. Alex was weak. I knew he couldn't live with a brain tumour. So I made him think he might have one. He didn't realise it was my suggestion. I even persuaded him to clean the gun so there were no fingerprints on it. It was so easy. Much too easy.'

He looked at Eliot for a moment.

'The funny thing is that Lisa's left me anyway,' he said with a sound that was almost like a laugh.

'What did you tell him you wanted to sell, Doctor?' Eliot asked quietly.

'The mirror in my sitting room. It's the nicest thing I own.'

He looked at Eliot for a moment.

'I didn't think you'd realise, Inspector,' he said with a small smile. 'You didn't seem especially intelligent.'

Eliot did not reply.

Before he was taken to the cells, Wilver asked one more question.

'What's Sam going to do now?' he said. But he did not seem to expect an answer.

Eliot felt very tired. He was glad the case was over. Except for Amanda Grant, he had seen enough of Forley's friends. The interview had left a very unpleasant taste in his mouth. Men like Wilver believed they could control everything. How could he seriously believe that Forley's death would solve his son's problems? Especially as Sam had loved Forley so much. Eliot felt very sorry for the boy. He knew that Wilver had really been thinking of himself. Love can be so blind, he thought.

He looked across the room. Bowen's head was

bent over his notes, his dark curly hair hiding the black circles under his eyes. He had spent all night finishing Forley's diary. Eliot smiled to himself. He wondered how long it would be before Bowen phoned Linda Scott. Would she be free, and would she be interested in him? This time maybe he would be lucky. Eliot hoped so. But in life you could never be sure of anything.

# After reading

## 读后活动

1. At the end, Eliot thinks: 'But in life you could never be sure of anything.' Do you agree?
2. Do you think *But Was It Murder?* is a good title? Make up a different title.
3. Dr Wilver, Ronald and Catherine Crowther have all committed crimes. How should they be punished?
4. Which characters do you like best in the story?
5. Do you think Bowen will be lucky in love? Write an extra chapter, including Bowen's first date with Linda Scott.
6. Imagine ten years have passed. Write a letter from Philip Wilver to his son Sam telling him the truth about what he did.
7. Make a quiz for the other students to do, e.g. write some True/False questions.

# Learning guide | 学习指导

## Chapter 1

### New words 生词

- admit /ədˈmɪt/ *v.* 承认
- automatically /ˌɔːtəˈmætɪkli/ *ad.* 自动地
- constable /ˈkʌnstəbl/ *n.* 警员
- detective /dɪˈtektɪv/ *n.* 侦探，刑警
- doorway /ˈdɔːweɪ/ *n.* 门口
- escape /ɪˈskeɪp/ *v.* 逃离
- inspector /ɪnˈspektə(r)/ *n.* 督察
- inviting /ɪnˈvaɪtɪŋ/ *a.* 吸引人的
- madness /ˈmædnəs/ *n.* 疯狂
- pathologist /pəˈθɒlədʒɪst/ *n.* 病理学家
- sigh /saɪ/ *v.* 叹气
- stick /stɪk/ *v.* 卡住，难以移动

### Phrases & expressions 短语和表达

- at least 至少
- be crazy about ... 对……痴迷
- drunk driving 醉酒驾车
- pick up (the phone) 接（电话）
- put down (the phone) 挂掉（电话）
- traffic jam 交通堵塞

## Cultural notes 文化点滴

• inspector: 督察。一种警衔。英国的警衔由低到高主要有：constable（警员）、sergeant（警长）、inspector（督察）、superintendent（警司）、commissioner（警务处长）等。

• West Ham: 西汉姆。全称为西汉姆联足球俱乐部（West Ham United Football Club），是英格兰超级联赛的球队之一、英格兰传统足球俱乐部，位于伦敦纽汉区，成立于 1895 年。

## Reading exercise 阅读练习

Match the beginnings and endings.

_______ 1) Eliot was planning to

_______ 2) Bowen phoned to tell him about

_______ 3) Eliot was annoyed about

_______ 4) Eliot knew the journey

_______ 5) Eliot phoned Brighton

a) a death in the Blackheath area.

b) not being able to spend the weekend with his family.

c) and gave his good wishes to his family.

d) have a beer on the way home.

e) would take ages in the heavy traffic.

# Chapter 2

## New words 生词

• antique /æn'ti:k/ *a.* 古老的

- divorce /dɪˈvɔːs/ *v.* 离婚
- explode /ɪkˈspləʊd/ *v.* 爆炸
- fireplace /ˈfaɪəpleɪs/ *n.* 壁炉
- impatiently /ɪmˈpeɪʃntli/ *ad.* 不耐烦地
- obviously /ˈɒbviəsli/ *ad.* 明显地
- Persian /ˈpɜːʃn/ *a.* 波斯的
- sheet /ʃiːt/ *n.* 纸张；薄片；床单
- siren /ˈsaɪrən/ *n.* 汽笛
- stretch /stretʃ/ *v.* 伸展
- suicide /ˈsuːɪsaɪd/ *n.* 自杀
- wander /ˈwɒndə(r)/ *v.* 漫步

## Phrases & expressions 短语和表达

- have a high opinion of ... 对……评价高
- have a word with ... 和……交谈
- in one’s thirties 在某人三十多岁
- look forward to doing sth. 期待做某事
- switch on ... 打开……
- turn off 拐出（某条路）

## Cultural notes 文化点滴

- Cambridge University: 剑桥大学。一所坐落于英国剑桥的书院联邦制大学，是世界著名的研究型大学之一。剑桥大学为英国历史第二悠久的大学，其前身是一个于 1209 年成立的学者协会 。这些学者本为牛津大学的一员，但后来因为与牛津郡民发生冲突而移居至此。剑桥和牛津这两所古老的大学在办学模式等多方面都非常相似，经常争夺全英最佳学府的声誉。

- Guy Fawkes Day: 盖伊·福克斯日。英国的传统节日，时间为每年的 11 月 5 日。这个节日是为了纪念"火药阴谋"这一历史事件。1605 年，天主教徒盖伊·福克斯及其同伙密谋炸毁位于伦敦威斯敏斯特的英国议会大厦。但阴谋被挫败了，盖伊·福克斯及其同党被以叛国罪处死。后来，人们在庆祝这个节日时，会自己制作"盖伊"——一个用旧衣服填充做成的假人，再把它放到篝火上焚烧。最后，绚丽的焰火燃放起来，代表历史上那场爆炸阴谋的粉碎。
- Mahler's Eighth Symphony: 马勒的《第八交响曲》。奥地利作曲家及指挥家古斯塔夫·马勒（Gustav Mahler）所创作的交响曲中最著名的一首。《第八交响曲》创作于 1906—1907 年，于 1910 年 9 月 12 日由马勒指挥在德国慕尼黑首演。参与这支交响曲演出的除了庞大的交响乐队，还有两个混声合唱队、一个童声合唱团、七位独唱演员，因此，此曲也被称为"千人交响曲"。

## Reading exercise 阅读练习

True or false?

a) Bowen is lucky in love.

b) Bowen is a good-looking man.

c) Eliot does not have a good opinion of Bowen.

d) Eliot recognised the face of the dead man.

e) The dead man had the musician's hands.

f) The pathologist was happy in his work.

# Chapter 3

## New words 生词

- arrange /əˈreɪndʒ/ *v.* 整理
- embarrassment /ɪmˈbærəsmənt/ *n.* 窘迫，尴尬
- explosion /ɪkˈspləʊʒn/ *n.* 爆炸
- lined /laɪnd/ *a.* 有皱纹的
- mug /mʌg/ *n.*（圆筒、有柄的）大杯
- single /ˈsɪŋgl/ *a.* 单身的
- sort /sɔːt/ *n.* 类别
- toothbrush /ˈtuːθbrʌʃ/ *n.* 牙刷
- unlocked /ˌʌnˈlɒkt/ *a.* 没有锁的

## Phrases & expressions 短语和表达

- care for ... 保养……，护理……
- pay (no) attention to ...（不）留意……
- shaving brush（修脸前涂抹肥皂用的）刮须刷

## Cultural note 文化点滴

- French windows: 落地窗。英语中有很多表达跟国家或民族相关，比如 French fries（炸马铃薯条）、go Dutch（各自付账，AA 制）、Dutch courage（酒后之勇）、Indian summer（秋季的和暖天气，小阳春；晚年的幸福时期）、Swiss roll（夹有果酱或奶油的卷筒夹心蛋糕）等，它们背后都蕴藏着有趣的文化典故。

## Reading exercise 阅读练习

Complete the summary.

Forley lived __________, but cared for his house more than most __________ men and had good __________ and money. Eliot spoke to Forley's __________. Mr Crowther was in late middle age but his wife was __________, beautiful and much __________. They hadn't seen Forley for a __________ but had been expecting him at __________ that afternoon. Mr Crowther said Forley was like a __________ to them.

# Chapter 4

## New words 生词

- accidental /ˌæksɪˈdentl/ *a.* 偶然的，意外的
- attached /əˈtætʃt/ *a.* 连在一起的
- bang /bæŋ/ *n.* 巨响
- gunshot /ˈɡʌnʃɒt/ *n.* 枪炮射击
- hand /hænd/ *v.* 传递，交给
- identify /aɪˈdentɪfaɪ/ *v.* 识别，辨认出
- relative /ˈrelətɪv/ *n.* 亲戚
- violent /ˈvaɪələnt/ *a.* 暴力的

## Phrases & expressions 短语和表达

- hold on 等一下
- not give it another thought 不放在心上
- salary rise 工资上涨

## Cultural note 文化点滴

• Royal Naval College: 英国皇家海军学院。英国培养海军初级军官的主要院校，被誉为英国海军军官的“摇篮”。该学院创建于1863年，设在英格兰德文郡的达特茅斯，故又称“达特茅斯皇家海军学院”。

## Reading exercise 阅读练习

Match the questions with the answers.

______ 1) ‘Then you think it looked like suicide?’

______ 2) ‘Can you tell us about Mr Forley’s job? You said he had a shop in Greenwich.’

______ 3) ‘You didn’t hear anything, did you, my dear?’

______ 4) ‘What time was this?’

______ 5) ‘Did he ever marry?’

a) ‘It must have been after three o’clock.’

b) ‘That’s impossible. Alex would not have killed himself.’

c) ‘No. He had a girlfriend, though – Amanda Grant.’

d) ‘Well, I do remember hearing a bang while you were out.’

e) ‘Forley Antiques. It’s one of those big antique furniture shops on Park Street ...’

# Chapter 5

## New words 生词

- alcohol /ˈælkəhɒl/ *n.* 酒；酒精
- brake /breɪk/ *v.* 刹车

- case /keɪs/ *n.* 案件
- comedy /ˈkɒmədi/ *n.* 喜剧
- crash /kræʃ/ *n.* 碰撞
- element /ˈelɪmənt/ *n.* 要素
- engine /ˈendʒɪn/ *n.* 发动机
- eventually /ɪˈventʃuəli/ *ad.* 终究，最后
- export /ɪkˈspɔːt/ *v.* 出口
- heating /ˈhiːtɪŋ/ *n.* 暖气设备
- overtake /ˌəʊvəˈteɪk/ *v.* 超车
- pavement /ˈpeɪvmənt/ *n.* 人行道
- pillow /ˈpɪləʊ/ *n.* 枕头
- professional /prəˈfeʃənl/ *n.* 专业人员
- queue /kjuː/ *v.* 排队
- recognise /ˈrekəgnaɪz/ *v.* 认出
- silver-grey /ˈsɪlvə(r) ˈgreɪ/ *a.* 银灰色的
- sweat /swet/ *n.* 汗水
- takeaway /ˈteɪkəweɪ/ *a.* 供应外带食物的
- wedding /ˈwedɪŋ/ *n.* 婚礼

## Phrases & expressions 短语和表达

- be mad about ... 迷恋……
- be successful with ... 在……方面成功
- only just 刚刚
- slow down 减速
- What does sb. see in sb. 不知道某人看上了某人什么

## Reading exercise 阅读练习

Look at the words *in italics*. Who is *she*, *he*?

a) *She* was certainly attractive, if you liked tall thin women ...

b) *He* had been coming to work with dark circles under his eyes recently.

c) But *he* seems quite ordinary. *He* must be rich, though ...

d) And what had *she* wanted to say about the gun?

e) *He* didn't seem to have left a note ...

# Chapter 6

## New words 生词

- bribe /braɪb/ *n.* 贿赂
- fingerprint /ˈfɪŋɡəprɪnt/ *n.* 指纹
- occasionally /əˈkeɪʒnəli/ *ad.* 偶尔
- pullover /ˈpʊləʊvə(r)/ *n.* 套衫
- rarely /ˈreəli/ *ad.* 很少
- toast /təʊst/ *n.* 烤面包
- unwilling /ʌnˈwɪlɪŋ/ *a.* 不愿意的

## Phrases & expressions 短语和表达

- in between 在中间
- show no sign of ... 没有……的迹象
- switch off ... 关掉……

## Cultural notes 文化点滴

- *Cutty Sark*: 卡蒂萨克号，现存的最古老的帆船，也是世界帆船史上航行速度最快的一艘船。它于 1869 年在苏格兰建成，主要用于运茶等海上贸易；现在位于英国泰晤士河旁的港口上，成了博物馆。“卡蒂萨克号”在 2007 年进行维护时失火，损坏严重，2012 年修复好后重新对外开放。
- Millennium Dome: 千禧穹顶。位于英国伦敦泰晤士河边的格林尼治半岛，占地 300 英亩，是英国为庆祝千禧年而建的建筑之一，整个建筑为穹庐形，12 根 100 米高的钢桅杆直刺苍穹。
- Old Royal Observatory: 老皇家天文台，也被称为“皇家格林尼治天文台（Royal Greenwich Observatory）”，始建于 1675 年，位于英国伦敦的格林尼治花园中，第二次世界大战后迁往萨塞克斯郡，但保留了“皇家格林尼治天文台”的名称。1884 年，国际子午线会议决定，通过皇家格林尼治天文台子午仪中心的经线为本初子午线。格林尼治子午线上的地方时被称为“格林尼治标准时间（GMT）”，这既是英国的标准时间，也是世界各地时间的参考标准。1997 年，皇家格林尼治天文台旧址被列为世界文化遗产。
- Queen's House: 皇后之屋。建于 1616—1635 年，是詹姆士一世为安妮皇后所建，后来成为继任国王查理一世的皇后玛丽亚钟爱的地方。这座精美小巧的白色两层建筑是英国第一栋帕拉迪奥风格的建筑。帕拉迪奥是文艺复兴末期意大利的建筑师，他的设计注重建筑外观的对称与和谐，同时考虑到内部使用功能。英国 17 世纪以后的建筑风格深受帕拉迪奥影响。

## Reading exercise 阅读练习

Put the events in the right order.

a) One look at Forley's hands was enough for her to be certain.

b) She didn't show any emotion until she saw the body.

c) Only the dead man's fingerprints had been found on the gun.

d) Amanda Grant agreed to identify the body.

e) Eliot and Bowen went to speak to Amanda Grant.

# Chapter 7

## New words 生词

- gently /ˈdʒentli/ *ad.* 轻轻地；温柔地；有礼貌地
- helplessly /ˈhelpləsli/ *ad.* 无助地
- intend /ɪnˈtend/ *v.* 意欲，打算
- jealous /ˈdʒeləs/ *a.* 嫉妒的
- pretend /prɪˈtend/ *v.* 假装
- sharply /ˈʃɑːpli/ *ad.* 尖锐地
- thoughtfully /ˈθɔːtfəli/ *ad.* 若有所思地
- truthfully /ˈtruːθfəli/ *ad.* 诚实地

## Phrases & expressions 短语和表达

- depend on ... 依靠……，依赖……
- for some reason 由于某种原因
- share interests with ... 和……有共同爱好
- ... without a word 一句话不说就……

## Cultural note 文化点滴

- have a doctor: 拥有一位家庭医生、私人医生。家庭医生制度在英国、美国等国家发展成熟，一些人看病先找自己的家庭医生。家庭医生是全科医生，提供个性化的医疗保健服务，使人们足不出户就能解决日常健康问题。

## Reading exercise 阅读练习

Complete the summary.

Amanda Grant had known Forley for almost ________ years. They had had an ________ about her ________ the last time they met. Amanda said Forley had shared ________ with Catherine Crowther, and had begun to find Ronald Crowther ________. Eliot wanted to ask if Amanda was ________ of Catherine, but didn't. Amanda also said that Forley had been having ________ and had been to hospital for ________.

# Chapter 8

## New words 生词

- answerphone /ˈɑːnsəfəʊn/ *n.* 自动应答录音电话
- bonfire /ˈbɒnfaɪə(r)/ *n.* 篝火
- criminal /ˈkrɪmɪnl/ *n.* 罪犯
- instruction /ɪnˈstrʌkʃn/ *n.* 指令
- pile /paɪl/ *v.* 堆积
- religion /rɪˈlɪdʒən/ *n.* 宗教
- religious /rɪˈlɪdʒəs/ *a.* 宗教的

- richness /ˈrɪtʃnəs/ *n.* 丰富
- sigh /saɪ/ *v.* 叹气

## Phrases & expressions 短语和表达

- blow up sth. 使某物爆炸
- have strong feelings for ... 对……有强烈的感情
- in sb.'s mind's eye 在某人心目中
- the day before 前一天

## Reading exercise 阅读练习

Match the beginnings and endings of the sentences.

______ 1) Eliot thought Amanda had strong feelings for Forley

______ 2) Bowen was interested to know what

______ 3) There was a message from a man called Philip –

______ 4) Bowen was surprised that

______ 5) Eliot knew Forley hadn't been killed for money

a) the same first name as Forley's doctor.

b) but there had been problems between them.

c) there was £2,200 in cash on the desk.

d) because the money had not been stolen.

e) Amanda and Catherine felt about each other.

## Cultural note 文化点滴

- Houses of Parliament: 议会大厦。又称“威斯敏斯特宫（Palace of Westminster）”，是英国议会（包括上议院和下议院）的所在地。威斯敏斯特宫是哥特式建筑的代表作之一，1987 年被列为世界文化遗产。威斯敏斯特厅是威斯敏斯特宫现存最为古老的部分，始建于 1097 年，曾用于王室加冕礼、国葬前追悼会的遗体陈列等重大仪式。

## Chapter 9

### New words 生词

- affair /əˈfeə(r)/ *n.* 风流韵事
- disappointment /ˌdɪsəˈpɔɪntmənt/ *n.* 失望
- liar /ˈlaɪə(r)/ *n.* 说谎者
- misunderstand /ˌmɪsʌndəˈstænd/ *v.* 误解
- navy-blue /ˈneɪvi ˈbluː/ *a.* 深蓝色的
- strengthen /ˈstreŋθn/ *v.* 加强
- tumour /ˈtjuːmə(r)/ *n.* 肿瘤

### Phrases & expressions 短语和表达

- commit suicide 自杀
- die of ... 死于……
- make up one's mind 下定决心
- take interest in ... 对……产生兴趣

### Reading exercises 阅读练习

1. Match the questions with the answers.

______ 1) 'You said yesterday that you didn't believe it was suicide. What made you so sure?'

______ 2) 'And was Mr Forley in a difficult situation?'

______ 3) 'Now, you mentioned a gun last night. Can you tell me more about it?'

_______ 4) 'Now, I understand Mr Forley had been worried about his health. Could you tell me about it?'

_______ 5) 'What was his relationship with Miss Grant like?'

a) '... He'd had a lot of headaches, and he took them very seriously.'

b) '... She didn't always understand him. It caused problems between them.'

c) 'Well, I could see he had something on his mind that he wouldn't talk about.'

d) 'I didn't know what I was saying yesterday, Inspector. Of course, it's possible that he killed himself.'

e) 'Did I? I was so shocked yesterday. I've forgotten what I said.'

2. You have now read half the book. Was it murder? Or was it suicide? What do you think?

## Chapter 10

### New words 生词

- move /muːv/ *n.* 行动
- routine /ruːˈtiːn/ *a.* 例行的，常规的 *n.* 例行程序

### Phrases & expressions 短语和表达

- appear to do sth. 表现出做某事
- be guilty of ... 犯有……罪
- call in at ... 顺路拜访……
- have a bad word 说坏话

- hold up sth. 举起某物
- stand side by side 并排站立
- work on ... 从事于……

## Reading exercise 阅读练习

Put the events in the right order.

a) Eliot felt sure the Crowthers were lying about the gun.

b) Bowen thought that Ronald Crowther might be frightened.

c) Linda Scott told the police that Forley had been worried and unhappy.

d) Mrs Crowther was embarrassed when Eliot asked about her painting.

e) Linda Scott said that Forley had taken £2,200 out of the shop.

# Chapter 11

## New words 生词

- ashtray /ˈæʃtreɪ/ *n.* 烟灰缸
- Greek /griːk/ *n.* 希腊语
- judgement /ˈdʒʌdʒmənt/ *n.* 判断
- Latin /ˈlætɪn/ *n.* 拉丁语
- persuade /pəˈsweɪd/ *v.* 劝说

## Phrases & expressions 短语和表达

- can't stop doing sth. 忍不住做某事
- cigarette end 烟头
- hold on to ... 紧紧抓住……，紧紧抱住……

### Reading exercise 阅读练习

True or false?

a) Eliot slept through most of the football match.

b) Bowen looked tired and stressed.

c) Forley's diary was not written in English.

d) Wilver's wife was relaxed and cheerful.

e) The Wilvers' sitting room was in an awful mess.

f) The tests showed there was something wrong with Forley.

## Chapter 12

### New word 生词

- surgery /ˈsɜːdʒəri/ *n.* 诊室，门诊处

### Phrases & expressions 短语和表达

- come round 拜访
- deep in thought 沉思中
- get rid of ... 摆脱……
- in sb.'s shoes 处于某人的境地

### Reading exercise 阅读练习

Look at the words *in italics*. Who is *he*, *you*, *she*?

a) *He* said *he* wanted my advice about something.

b) And would *you* say he was a weak man, sir?

c) *She*'s good-looking enough, but *she* obviously rules his life.

d) Be careful with the women *you* choose.

e) *He*'s hiding something from us, too.

## Chapter 13

### New words 生词

- brilliant /ˈbrɪliənt/ *a.* 精彩的
- complicated /ˈkɒmplɪkeɪtɪd/ *a.* 复杂的

### Phrases & expressions 短语和表达

- except for ... 除了……
- make a great effort to do sth. 非常努力地做某事
- stay up 熬夜

### Reading exercise 阅读练习

Eliot needs answers to these questions:

a) Why were the Crowthers not telling him the truth?

b) Had Catherine Crowther been having an affair with Forley?

c) What had made her suddenly change her style of painting?

d) And did anyone visit Forley after Wilver had left on Friday?

e) And what had Forley been so worried about? What do you think?

## Chapter 14

### New words 生词

- alibi /ˈæləbaɪ/ *n.* 不在场证明

- barman /ˈbɑːmən/ *n.* 酒吧男招待员
- forehead /ˈfɔːhed/ *n.* 额头

## Reading exercise 阅读练习

Complete the summary.

The pathologist's report said that Forley had been killed by a shot to the __________ and had died __________. There were no other signs of __________. He had been in good __________ but had been drinking. The time of death was between __________ and __________ Friday afternoon. Eliot now had to check who had an __________ for that time. Bowen was making slow progress on Forley's __________ as it was written in __________ and __________.

# Chapter 15

## New words 生词

- apparently /əˈpærəntli/ *ad.* 貌似，看来；显然
- suspect /səˈspekt/ *n.* 犯罪嫌疑人
- uncover /ʌnˈkʌvə(r)/ *v.* 揭露

## Reading exercise 阅读练习

Match the beginnings and endings.

_______ 1) Mrs Brook told the police that

_______ 2) Forley was with Catherine Crowther for an hour

_______ 3) Mrs Brook had once seen

_______ 4) Bowen discovered from the secret diary

_______ 5) The barman in the pub noticed Ronald Crowther

a) going for a walk at the time of Forley's death.

b) Forley had visited Catherine Crowther on Wednesday.

c) that Forley had been having an affair.

d) and looked very uncomfortable when he left.

e) Ronald Crowther cleaning a gun.

## Chapter 16

### New words 生词

- bullet /ˈbʊlɪt/ *n.* 子弹
- gentleness /ˈdʒentlnəs/ *n.* 彬彬有礼
- guilt /gɪlt/ *n.* 内疚
- jealousy /ˈdʒeləsi/ *n.* 嫉妒

### Reading exercise 阅读练习

Who ...

a) gave the gun to Forley?

b) were at the dinner party three weeks ago?

c) was surprised that Eliot wanted to ask more questions?

d) was having a secret affair with Forley?

e) was angry with Forley?

f) thought Catherine was finally telling the truth?

# Chapter 17

## New words 生词

- character /ˈkærəktə(r)/ *n.* 性格，个性
- unpack /ʌnˈpæk/ *v.* 打开行李取出东西

## Phrases & expressions 短语和表达

- at the earliest 最早
- cover sth. up 掩盖某事
- make a will 立下遗嘱

## Cultural note 文化点滴

- London City Airport: 伦敦城市机场。英国伦敦有五大机场，除了伦敦城市机场外，另外四个机场分别是：London Heathrow Airport（伦敦希思罗机场）、London Gatwick Airport（伦敦盖特威克机场）、London Stansted Airport（伦敦斯坦斯特德机场）以及 London Luton Airport（伦敦卢顿机场）。

## Reading exercises 阅读练习

1. Put the events in the right order.
   a) Amanda Grant told the police what she had done on Friday.
   b) Eliot started to think it was suicide, not murder.
   c) Micky, Eliot's son, helped him understand something.
   d) Bowen checked her story and knew she was not guilty.
   e) Eliot thought that Amanda Grant was the murderer.

2. 'Thanks, Micky, I understand it now.' What do you think Eliot understood?

## Chapter 18

### New words 生词

- cassette /kəˈset/ *n.* 盒式录音带
- cell /sel/ *n.* 牢房

### Reading exercise 阅读练习

Complete the summary.

Wilver phoned Forley on __________ to say he needed __________ and wanted to __________ something, which explained the __________ on Forley's desk. Also, Wilver __________ about the test results on Friday, saying Forley might have a __________ . Wilver knew about the __________ and was sure Forley would __________ himself. Wilver knew Lisa was having an __________ with Forley, but didn't want Sam to grow up without a __________.

# Translation
# 参考译文

# 死亡诊断

## 第 1 章　没去成女王之首酒吧

### 第5页

刑侦督察罗德·埃利奥特正看着雨水从他办公室的窗户上直流而下。他看了看手表，六点半。是时候离开办公桌上堆积如山的文件，去马路对面的女王之首酒吧了。

“但是只能喝一杯啤酒，”他告诉自己，“我可不想因为酒驾被某个初级警察拦住。那样我就得回家独守空房了。”

他正要离开办公室，电话响了。他不假思索地转过身去，拿起电话。他有五分期待来电话的会是他的妻子。

“对不起，打扰您了，长官，”刑侦警员杰米·鲍恩说，“我们遇到了一点儿麻烦。”

“我也有事，”埃利奥特说，“我不该当班了。去找梅里昂督察吧。”

“对不起，长官，”鲍恩说，“可是梅里昂督察还没有到。他打电话说他的车堵在了哈克尼区，很可能至少要一个小时才能到这儿。”

### 第6页

埃利奥特生气地敲了一下桌面。女王之首酒吧的灯看起来如此诱人。但是在下面的街道上，人们纷纷挤进商店的门口，试图躲避这场大雨。雨水倾泻到街道上，再被一排排缓慢驶离伦敦市中心的车溅起来。

“好吧，鲍恩，”他说，“那你还是告诉我吧。是什么案件？”

“我们刚刚收到一份死亡报告，长官，并且现场有一把枪。”

这是埃利奥特最不想听到的事情。他的心情一整天都不好。他通常喜欢星期五是因为转眼就是周末，在周末他可以花时间跟他的妻子萨莉还有 8 岁大的儿子米基在一起。米基痴迷足球，埃利奥特周六总是带他去看西汉姆的主场比赛。但是，这个周末将会无法如常了。埃利奥特不得不工作，萨莉带着米基去了布赖顿她父母的家里，要住两个晚上。早上他和萨莉吵了架。

“别喊了，”她说，“你生气就是因为你不想让我们走。你为什么不能承认？”

## 第7页

她是正确的，但是正是明白这点让他更生气。他没跟她说再见就离开了家。

他尝试拨了几次电话想道歉，但是没有人接电话。这会儿她应该在她父母家，并且她不能当着大家的面和他打电话，因为她父母会听见。

“从早上醒来那刻我就知道今天会是糟糕的一天，”他告诉鲍恩，“好吧。我们必须得去了。在哪儿？”

“恐怕是在布莱克希思，长官。”

埃利奥特叹了一口气。布莱克希思离新十字警察局只有六千米远，但在星期五晚上的这个时候，交通太拥堵了，以至于这段路程将花去超过一个小时的时间。

埃利奥特想不出比这更糟糕的度过周五晚上的方式了，特别是他第二天早上还得早早地到办公室。为什么大家都想在同一时间离开伦敦呢？总有那么一天整个城市都将陷入无尽的交通拥堵之中。现在的交通运行已经比一百年前都慢了，简直令人发疯！

“十分钟后在楼下等我，鲍恩，”他说，“哦，必须有医学报告。确定一下是否有人通知了医生和病理学家。”

● 第8页

埃利奥特从窗前转过身来。还好，至少萨莉和米基没有在家等着他。他最好现在给他们打电话，这可能是他今晚最后的时机了。

萨莉的父亲拿起电话：“你好，罗德。真遗憾你来不了这儿，这里天气非常好。工作怎么样啊？”

埃利奥特尽量客气地闲聊了几分钟，然后说要和萨莉讲话。

“恐怕她不在家里，”她爸爸说，“她带米基出去散步了。他迫不及待地要去看海。要给她留口信吗？”埃利奥特无法相信他运气这么糟。

“就说他们平安到达我很开心，”他说，“然后告诉她我爱她。明天我再打电话。”

他放下电话，最后看了一眼女王之首酒吧。路上的车辆好像几乎没有动过。还好，至少他能让鲍恩来开车。

## 第 2 章　死亡的颜色

● 第9页

车前进了几米，就又停了。鲍恩一开始就开了蓝灯和警笛，以便其他司机能让他们过去。但是已经没有让他们开过去的空档了，他们还差点儿引起了两起交通事故。

这会儿他们算是到布莱克希思了。雨停了，但交通状况似乎变得越来越糟糕了。

布莱克希思村是伦敦东南部最漂亮、绿化最好的地区之一。在景色宜人的山坡上有几条狭窄的街道，街道上坐落着不落俗套的房舍和许多饭馆。大片的草地把村庄与主路分开。在这里，孩子们玩耍，恋人们漫步，一家人遛着狗散步。

明天晚上这里将会人山人海，因为明天是11月5日——盖伊·福克斯日。成千上万的人不是在自己家的院子里开派对，就是来布莱克希思看烟花表演。其中有些派对似乎已经开始了。烟花在人们上空绽放，空中到处都是烟花的声音和五彩的颜色。

## 第10页

想到儿子，埃利奥特猛地感到一阵心痛。明天米基会有多兴奋啊。埃利奥特本来很想带他到这里来。

现在他却得让自己想着工作。

“你对这起命案知道多少?”他问鲍恩。

“不多，长官。死者是白人，男性，三十多岁。”

“我估计我们到达现场后会发现更多线索。如果我们确实能到的话，鲍恩。”埃利奥特不耐烦地加了一句。

“抱歉，长官。我正在尽全力呢。”鲍恩说。

埃利奥特想知道鲍恩看到死者尸体时会有怎样的感受。即使是对于工作了多年的他来说，这活儿也从来都不好干，虽然他已经变得坚强了很多。

鲍恩28岁，比埃利奥特小10岁，入警以来就一直和他搭班。他的父母很有钱，并且他是剑桥大学毕业的。这样的背景最初让埃利奥特不放心。但是鲍恩诚实又聪明，是个好警察。埃利奥特现在对他评价颇高，虽然他不经常表现出来。

但是关于鲍恩，埃利奥特有一件事不明白：他总是爱上不合适的女人。她们要么是已婚，要么是对他不感兴趣，要么是完全不正常。最近鲍恩和埃利奥特一起在车里的时候，他开始向埃利奥特寻求建议。

## 第11页

“受了那么多教育，还不会找女朋友。真是浪费了！”埃利奥特心想，“再说，他也不难看，长着一双黑黑的眼睛，满头黑色卷发。”

埃利奥特明白他自己幸福地结了婚是多么幸运。他同情鲍恩，也因为那天早上和萨莉吵嘴而对自己气恼。他真希望他打电话那会儿她正好在。

终于他们转下了主路，在一条静谧街道的尽头处一幢小巧却漂亮的18世纪的房子外面停下了。所有窗户的灯都亮着。埃利奥特从车里下来，抻了抻腿。正常来说，他应该会很期待看看如此漂亮的房子内部的。

一位年轻的警察开了门。他看起来脸色苍白，似乎非常高兴见到他们。

“晚上好，长官。晚上好，长官。”他边说边逐一打量着他们二人。“我叫德鲁伊特。那个，呃，尸体在那边，从这边过去。”

他们跟着他，穿过铺着深红色波斯地毯的大厅，经过几级漂亮的木楼梯，进入了后面的起居室。壁炉里烧着火，矮桌上几盏灯发出柔和的光，映在窗帘、墙壁和古董家具上。窗边有一架开着盖子的钢琴，上面放着乐谱和半玻璃杯红酒。

## 第12页

埃利奥特的注意力被一把扶手椅旁边墙上的一片暗色斑块吸引了过去。它和大厅的地毯是一样的颜色。乍一看，它似乎是这个房间里唯一难看的东西。但随后埃利奥特低头看了看椅子，又迅速地转移了视线。

那是一具男人的尸体。不过他只能从它的外形和衣着上判断那是一具男尸，从现存的面孔不足以判断出性别。尸体坐在一把椅子上，背对着窗户。一把枪躺在旁边的地板上。

埃利奥特让自己又看了一眼。(尸体的) 双手修长，手指纤细，指形优美——弹钢琴的手。在右手的第三根手指上戴着一枚沉甸甸的金戒指。这么看来他还未婚，或者可能是离婚了。他的衣服看起来价格不菲，正如你可以想象到的住这种房子人的样子。

短短的几秒里，这些想法在埃利奥特的脑海里闪现。鲍恩已拿出了笔记本，开始向德鲁伊特提问了。

## 第13页

“鲍恩现在变得同我一样坚强了，”埃利奥特想，“不像那位年轻的德鲁伊特。他那脸色惨白如纸。”

“知道他是谁吗?”鲍恩问德鲁伊特。

德鲁伊特明显说话有些费劲儿。“嗯，长官，”最后他说，“这幢房子属于一位叫亚历克斯·福尔利的先生。他的邻居给我们打的电话，克劳瑟先生和太太，他们住在隔壁。周五他通常会和他们喝茶。可是今天下午他没来，他们就有些担心，因为他一直感觉自己身体不舒服。他没有来应门铃开门，所以他们就进了他家的后花园，透过窗户看到了他。医生已经来过又走了，长官。”

## 第14页

“是的，”鲍恩说，“他不用待太久。任谁都能看得出这个人死了。”

“稍后我们会和克劳瑟夫妇谈一下，”埃利奥特说，“我最好在这儿等到病理学家来。鲍恩，你和其他的邻居谈谈怎么样？看看他们能否告诉我们一些有趣的事情。”

门铃响了，又进来两名警察，开始给尸体照相。但是又过了半个小时，病理学家才到。他又矮又胖但很开朗，看起来好像没有什么可以让他烦恼。

“你好，埃利奥特。很高兴又见到你了。抱歉，过了这么长时间才到。交通状况太糟糕了。我估计都是因为这些盖伊·福克斯之夜的派对。我不明白他们为什么不能等到明天呢。不过凡事都有好的一面。我在来这儿的路上终于听完了马勒的《第八交响乐》，非常棒的录音。人生苦短，没空儿烦忧。你不赞同吗，埃利奥特？”

## 第15页

埃利奥特没有回答。

“我确信他会赞同我的，如果他能表达的话，”这位病理学家兴致勃勃地指着椅子上的尸体说道，“当然，除非他是自杀的。好了，我得检查一下他了。我猜你们不想一晚上都待在这里闲聊吧。”

他打开他的包，而埃利奥特决定到外面去。

# 第3章　朋友而已

## 第16页

埃利奥特在房子四周走了走。花园是精心打理过的，这点甚至在夜色中都看得出来。草坪修剪过了，晚季玫瑰在两边的墙上正开着花，石头铺成的小路干净而又整洁。起居室的窗户是落地窗，可以像门一样打开，通向外面的花园。

“多宜人的房间。在夏天就更完美了。”他想着。

自然而然地，他走向了落地窗，试图打开它们。他相当惊奇地发现窗子没有上锁。

“我猜德鲁伊特就是从这儿进来的，”他想着，“不过，我还是想知道为什么它们会是开着的。现在已不是欣赏花园的时节了。但或许这也并不意味着什么，有些人喜欢在各种天气里出去看他们的玫瑰。”他看到花园的后墙上有一道门，看起来是新装的。在他们自己的花园里萨莉也想要一道这样的门，这样搬植物时就不用穿过房子了。

他回到房子里面，看了每一个房间。一看到浴室他就知道福尔利是独居的。一支牙刷立在一个马克杯里，旁边是一把修面刷，一面墙上的吊环里搭着一条毛巾。埃利奥特能看到在毛巾的一角有字母 AF。其他的房间都跟起居室一样布置得漂漂亮亮。很明显福尔利非常在意他的房子，比很多单身汉要在意得多。

## 第17页

“一个品位很高还很有钱的男人，”埃利奥特想，“一个幸运的男人。不过他的幸运就到今天为止了。我想知道其他人怎么看待他的幸运。”

他从楼梯上走下来，又等了一会儿，直到病理学家完成了他的工作。

“现在您能告诉我一些情况了吗？”他问他。

“嗯，我认为他刚死不久。但是我说不出更多的了，得等我好好地检验了再说。还有，我想您得等到周一才能拿到报告，恐怕我无法告诉您确切时间。这段时间我们很忙，活儿越来越多，但是还在裁员。世界都疯了。但是我知道您不介意等待，埃利奥特。您有家室，对吧？周末您还有很多充满乐趣的事情可以去考虑。”

他微笑着走出了门，这时鲍恩走了进来。

“你发现什么有意思的线索了吗？”埃利奥特问道。

## 第18页

“没什么发现，长官，”鲍恩说，“很多人都出门了。我交谈过的人都是最近刚搬过来的，似乎对他一点儿都不了解。有几个人提到他们有时候看到一个女人在这里，但是没有人对他感兴趣。他们谁都不知道他是做什么工作的。”

“城里人！”埃利奥特说道，“他们不关心自己的邻居。要不是克劳瑟夫妇给我们打电话，等到有人注意到事情不对的时候，他可能已经在这儿躺上好几个星期了。好吧，现在我们还是四处走走，然后去拜访一下他们夫妇。”

埃利奥特觉得20号房子没有福尔利的那么漂亮，不过前门周围种了玫瑰花，而且房前的花园比埃利奥特自己家的要大。如果有人给他这么一幢房子，他肯定不会拒绝。他们走上门前小径，按了门铃，没有注意他们周围正在燃放的烟花。

克劳瑟先生立刻打开了门。他满头白发，接近老年。他站得很直，这让他看起来比实际要高。他的脸上满是皱纹，但是看起来很健壮，尽管他的手在发抖。

“可怜的亚历克斯遭遇了什么？”他问。

## 第19页

“先生，我们还不知道，”埃利奥特说，“但是我们想问您和您妻子一些问题。”

克劳瑟努力控制好自己，然后领着他们进入了一间宽敞的起居室。埃利奥特的注意力被一面挂满了画的墙吸引了过去。那些画呈现的是几种颜色很有趣的交织，主要是蓝色和绿色，并且很明显是同一个人所画。克劳瑟先生介绍了他的妻子凯瑟琳，埃利奥特立刻觉得她就是那位画家。

她是一个漂亮的女人，金发碧眼，眼睛生得好看。很难判断她的年龄，但是她肯定比她的丈夫年轻得多。埃利奥特猜她四十多岁。她面无血色，但是她还是足够冷静地回答了他的问题。一个内心强大又聪慧的女人，埃利奥特想。

“不，督察先生，从一星期前我们就没有见过亚历克斯了，”她告诉他说，“我们通常在每个星期五下午聚一下，要么在这儿，要么在他家。我们这样的交往已经很多年了。今天早上他从他位于格林尼治的店里打电话说要过来。我和他打算合奏几曲。我们经常那么做，这是一种令人愉悦的打发周末的方式。”

“我相信是挺愉悦的。”埃利奥特说着，想起了他自己的那些个星期五下午。他转向她的丈夫。

## 第20页

“您认识福尔利先生很长时间了吗，先生？”

“让我想想。从他搬到这里到现在，肯定有差不多十五年了。那时大约是他大学毕业一年以后，他母亲刚刚去世。她很有钱，并且把钱全都留给了亚历克斯。她的去世让他成了一个很富裕的年轻人。”

“我明白了。”埃利奥特说。他让克劳瑟接着说。

“刚来的时候，亚历克斯很不开心，”他开始讲了起来，“他母亲之前病了一段时间。那是一种让人久卧病榻又很难受的疾病，他照顾着她。他父亲早几年就去世了，她和亚历克斯相依为命。总之，他到这里的时候，没有剩下什么亲人了。我们自己也没有孩子，督察先生，对我们来说他就像我们的儿子。”

福尔利和克劳瑟太太之间的年龄差距不会很大。如果像大多数人一样，福尔利 21 岁从大学毕业，他现在应该是 37 岁。对那样年纪的一个男人，她真的有当母亲的感觉吗？埃利奥特看了看克劳瑟太太，在她的脸上看到些许尴尬。

“你们本来预计他今天下午什么时候会来？”他问道。

### 第21页

“他通常四点左右来，”她的声音变了，“我无法在说到他的时候用过去时。我无法相信他再也不会来了。”

她把脸埋到双手里，无声地哭泣起来。

## 第 4 章　枪声

### 第22页

“但是布莱克希思不是一个暴力横行的地方，督察先生，”克劳瑟先生说，“我们已经在这里住了 30 年了，像这样的事情以前还未曾发生过。当然有时候会有几起盗窃，但是从来没有谋杀案。我们一直感觉在这里非常安全。”

埃利奥特想说谋杀可能发生在任何地方，甚至是在最让人安心的地方。但是他只是说：“等一下，先生，我们还不知道这是不是一起谋杀案。”

“这么说您认为看起来像自杀？”克劳瑟先生问道。

“那不可能，”他的妻子说，“亚历克斯不会自杀的。他能有什么理由自杀呢？”

“我还没有任何判断，克劳瑟先生，”埃利奥特回答道，“我只是必须考虑到所有的可能性，包括意外死亡。”

“哦，那把枪。”克劳瑟太太开口道。然后她又不说了，飞快地瞄了她的丈夫一眼。

## 第23页

一阵沉默，接着埃利奥特继续他的话题。

“您能给我们讲讲福尔利先生的工作吗？”他问道，“您提到他在格林尼治开了一家商店。”

“福尔利古董店，”她回答道，“是帕克大街上的大型古董家具商店之一，在皇家海军学院附近。您一定知道的。”

埃利奥特曾经去过那里一次，那时他刚结婚，萨莉要过生日。他看到橱窗里有一张小桌子，他觉得她会喜欢的。他刚涨了工资，他觉得自己或许能买得起。但是当他听到价格时真的吓了一跳。年轻的女店员让他感到很局促，然后他匆忙地离开了。

“是的，我进去过，”他回答说，“但是我不记得见过福尔利先生。”

“哦，他在那儿待的时间不多，”克劳瑟太太说，“他不用在那儿。他只负责选家具。店里有一位经理和一位兼职的店员，他们来做主要的工作。”

她在谈论福尔利时又使用现在时了，好像她不敢相信他死了。她和她丈夫两个人看起来都很疲倦。今天晚上埃利奥特不会从他们那儿得到太多有用的信息了。

“今天我们不会待很长时间，”他说，“但是恐怕我们明天还得再来一趟。现在我只想再弄清楚一两件事。今天下午你们注意到什么不寻常的事情了吗？”

## 第24页

两家的房子不是连幢，而且都有厚厚的墙。但是也有可能，这边能听到隔壁的一声枪响。

“恐怕我帮不到您，督察先生，”克劳瑟先生说，“今天下午大部分时间我都在外面。午饭后我像平常一样出去散步了，但是我直到大概四点十分才回来。亲爱的，你没听到什么动静，是吧？”他问他的妻子。

她似乎正在仔细地斟酌自己的用词。“嗯，你在外面的时候，我确实记得听到了‘砰’的一声。我正在工作，所以当时我也没多想。我是画画儿的，督察先生，我工作时得聚精会神。现在还有那么多烟花，我就没有多想。但是我觉得在下午那个不当不正的时候听到放烟花的声音是相当不寻常的。”

“那时是什么时间？”埃利奥特问道。

“肯定是三点钟以后了，”她说道，“我是三点开始画的。可能在三点半左右。”

“您当时在哪儿？”他问道。

## 第25页

“我楼上的前屋，”她回答道，“从那里您能看到亚历克斯家的前门。哦，为什么当时我没有多留点儿心呢？如果有人从房子里出来，我是可以看到他们的。”

“除非他们是从落地窗离开的，”埃利奥特说，“现在，恐怕我们得找人来辨认遗体，确认一下那就是福尔利先生。您告诉过我们他母亲去世以后他就没有亲人了。他结过婚吗？”

克劳瑟太太用她的手捂着脸。她的丈夫用一只手臂搂着她，替她回答。

“没有。不过，他有一个女朋友——阿曼达·格兰特。我一直觉得将来某一天他们会结婚的。我们把她的地址放在什么地方了。我去把它取来。”

他回到这个房间后，把地址递给了埃利奥特。

“请不要联系格兰特小姐，”埃利奥特说，“我们亲自来告诉她这个消息。”

埃利奥特向鲍恩点头示意，然后他们两人都站了起来。他们那晚想要的全部信息都拿到了。

## 第 5 章　新十字警察局的夜晚

### 第26页

“我不明白的是，”等他们又上了车，鲍恩说道，“为什么那么漂亮的一个女人会嫁给一个比自己大那么多的男人。她看中他什么了？”

埃利奥特没有回答。在他十年的婚姻期间，他也经常把萨莉作为对象问自己同样的问题。但是他意识到这个年轻人问这个问题是有他自己的出发点的。鲍恩真正想知道的是为什么有些男人能成功地处理好与女人的关系，而他自己却做不到。埃利奥特不知道原因。就是凭运气吧，他想，还有就是被适合自己的女人吸引到。

埃利奥特见过一两次鲍恩的最新一任女友，她是他在一次婚礼上遇到的一位摄影师。当然她很有魅力，如果你喜欢瘦高的女子的话。但是她看起来有些冷酷。他们俩的关系恶化已经有一段时间了，而且她已经不回他的电话了，但是鲍恩仍然很迷恋她。最近他总是眼下带着黑眼圈来上班，有两回埃利奥特已经不得不因为上班迟到的事找他谈话了。

## 第27页

“看得出来克劳瑟对他的妻子很着迷，”鲍恩说，“但是她对他是怎样的感觉呢？他们俩简直是天壤之别啊。她擅长音乐而且会画画儿。您看到墙上那些精彩的画作了吗？但是他似乎相当普通。不过，他一定很有钱，才能住在那样一幢房子里。”

埃利奥特让他继续说。想着克劳瑟夫妇的事总比去想那个死者更令人愉快，至少他们活着，而且还有可以辨别的脸庞。克劳瑟太太似乎和福尔利特别亲近。他很想知道关于这件事情她的丈夫是怎么看的。还有，关于那把枪，她想说什么？

很多的问题填满了他的脑海，它们终将需要答案。但是他尽量不去猜测答案会是什么。这个案子才刚刚开始，他还不知道所有的事实。让大脑保持尽可能开放的状态很重要。

当然，这可能并不是一件很难办的案子。他们可能会发现福尔利是自杀的。他似乎没有留下任何字条，但是现如今这也不算太不寻常。埃利奥特希望病理学家的报告不会让他们等太久。

## 第28页

回新十字警察局的路好走些了。现在路上的车少多了，并且他们只遇到了一次红灯。埃利奥特想，他甚至可能来得及到家看新闻。

过了布莱克希思山之后，鲍恩得更加注意路况了。这会儿在伦敦很多地方开车就像赛车一样，因为司机们都想方设法尽可能地互相超车。而且就算见到警车，他们也常常不减速。

突然，鲍恩不得不刹车以免撞车。一辆银灰色的奔驰车没开车灯，停在路中间，发动机还响着。

“这片儿的小子们干的！”埃利奥特说，“他们根本不知道危险。因为没人管他们。我想偷车是他们唯一找乐子的方式，至少是在他们够年龄卖毒品之前。”

前一周，他在一辆被偷的车上抓了两个男孩儿。当警方打去电话的时候，他俩的父亲还在看足球赛，而且他很生气，因为他不得不在比赛结束前去一趟警察局。这两个男孩儿被给予了严正警告，然后就被放了。但是刚过了两个小时，他们就又回到了警察局，脸上还带着笑。刚一到家，他们就直接出去又偷了一辆车。

## 第29页

如今这样的事情发生得越来越多了，这让埃利奥特很担心。年纪小的那个男孩儿刚十岁，只比米基大两岁。那样一个孩子还有什么希望？

一直以来，他努力保护米基不受城市生活恶劣因素的影响。但是，他不知道这还能延续多久。在新十字区，男孩子们得通过打架或犯罪来显示自己的强大。埃利奥特为他文质彬彬的儿子感到担忧。很长时间以来，他和萨莉一直商量着把家搬到一个更安全的地区去。下次到布莱克希思的话，他必须看看房价去。

二十分钟以后来了一名警察，把奔驰车开走了。

“车主会很高兴，他的车失而复得了，”鲍恩说，“他运气不错，车没有被职业小偷儿偷走，不然他就再也见不到它了。”

现在他们已经开过金史密斯学院。人行道上挤满了年轻人，他们或是在外卖餐厅外面等候，或是排队等着进入音乐俱乐部。女孩儿们穿着轻薄的裙子和外套，看起来很冷。这情景让埃利奥特想打开车里的暖风。他庆幸米基是个男孩儿。如果他有个女儿，他知道自己对她的担忧会更多。

## 第30页

当他进警察局去汇报情况的时候，警察局里特别拥挤。周五和周六的晚上总是最忙的。年轻人喝了太多的酒，而且很多人从早餐起除了一份三明治以外，就几乎没有吃什么东西。他们变得吵闹和暴力一点儿也不意外，打架斗殴是常事。“英国特色的问题，”埃利奥特想，“我们以此闻名。在假期和足球比赛期间，我们甚至还对国外输出这个特色呢。”

他从一家印度餐馆里买了一份外卖，然后开车回家了。新闻刚刚播完，他开始看一档喜剧节目。他一直喜欢看这个节目，但是今天节目里的笑话似乎不那么好笑。大概是因为他累了。他度过了如此漫长的一天。

正常情况下，埃利奥特的头一挨着枕头就能睡着，然后他会在八个小时后准时醒来，而且会感觉精力充沛。但是今晚他不断地翻来翻去，无法放松下来。当睡意终于到来的时候，他睡得也不踏实。

他梦见米基和萨莉坐在一辆被偷的奔驰车的后排座位上。一把枪放在前排司机旁边的座椅上。那个男人开得越来越快，埃利奥特惊恐地看着。他冲他吼着要他停车。那个男人没有减速却突然把头转了过来，埃利奥特没有看到人脸，只看到了血。埃利奥特醒来时浑身是汗。

# 第 6 章 辨认尸体

## 第32页

埃利奥特 7 点 45 分醒来，阳光正照在他的脸上。在清晨，事情似乎总会变好，这真神奇。昨晚的担忧已经完全消失了，他期待着接下来的这一天。

他麻利地洗了一个澡，然后下楼去信箱里取报纸。报纸头版充斥着政治贿赂的新闻。他一边兴致十足地读着报纸，一边喝着咖啡、吃着烤面包。换换格调，安静地吃顿早餐真不错。不过他也琢磨着什么时间可以给萨莉打电话。现在太早了，他会吵醒她的父母的。

他对听到她声音的渴望令人惊讶。在他们十年的婚姻里，他有时候不得不出远门工作。因为次数不多，他没有在意。但是她几乎没有把他一个人留下来的时候，他想念她。他猜这就是他睡得特别不踏实的原因。

## 第33页

在警察局，鲍恩正在他的办公室外面等他。

“有没有进展？”埃利奥特问道。

“嗯，长官，我们刚刚听说在房子里有多个人的指纹。但是在枪上只有死者的指纹。”

“没有多大帮助，”埃利奥特说，“这案子仍然有可能是自杀，也可能是一场意外，还有可能是谋杀。可能是有人向他开了枪，把枪擦干净，然后把它放到了他的手里，这样看起来像是自杀。好吧，我们最好去见一下阿曼达·格兰特，然后带她来看一下遗体。之后我们再去拜访克劳瑟夫妇。”

阿曼达·格兰特住在格林尼治，格林尼治在新十字区和布莱克希思区的中间。埃利奥特想早点儿动身，尽可能避开拥挤的人群。

每天有成千上万名游客从伦敦市中心到这里来。很多游客是去参观千禧穹顶的，而另一些游客是来看格林尼治的名胜古迹的：皇后之屋、老皇家天文台和“卡蒂萨克号”帆船——19 世纪从中国运输茶叶过来的最快的船。一到星期六，游客与来自伦敦其他区域的人们混在一起。他们游览公园，逛城镇周边的各种市场，在那里你几乎可以买到任何东西，无论新旧。

## 第34页

鲍恩不得不把车停在离阿曼达·格兰特的住所稍远的地方。她的房子不在路边，却可以直接望见对面的河，和小河只隔着她的花园和一条公共小路。房子很小，但是很漂亮。

“这里真是安静，我们几乎就像在乡间了，”埃利奥特说，“可是我们从格林尼治的中心区过来只用了几分钟。我想知道这幢房子值多少钱。肯定是我负担不起的一大笔钱。”

门开了，开门的是一位留着黑色短发、二十八九岁的女人，她穿着牛仔裤和一件颜色鲜亮的长套衫。她的脸色看起来相当苍白而疲惫。她没有凯瑟琳·克劳瑟那么美，但是她有一张迷人的面庞。埃利奥特想不起来他以前在哪里见过她。

“早上好，”埃利奥特说，“我是刑侦督察埃利奥特，这位是刑侦警员鲍恩。我们想要和阿曼达·格兰特谈谈，如果她在家的话。”

“我就是阿曼达·格兰特，”她回答道，她的声音异常低沉，“您需要我做什么，督察先生？”

“我们可以进去吗，格兰特小姐？”埃利奥特问道，“在屋里谈话会更轻松些。”

## 第36页

她看上去有些吃惊，但还是平静地邀请他们进来了。前门打开直接就是一间起居室，鲜艳的窗帘和地毯给人一种温暖的感觉。一只猫正在椅子上舔着毛。埃利奥特透过窗户可以看到河边的千禧穹顶上黄白相间的色块。在它的前面一艘小船慢慢地驶向格林尼治的中心区。在一张铺满了纸张和书本的写字台旁边有一台 CD 唱机，唱机里播放着钢琴曲。在写字台的一端，一枝玫瑰插在一个玻璃花瓶里。埃利奥特感觉很不愿意把死亡和枪的话题带进这间宁静的房间里。

他说话的时候，她什么都没有说，之后很长一段时间也没说什么。

“我猜想您是想要我去辨认尸体，”最后她说，“显然您需要确定他就是亚历克斯。”她的脸上没有流露出任何显现她内心感受的表情。

埃利奥特想知道他们还会在福尔利的生活中找到多少位这样坚强又聪慧的女人。

“是的，恐怕是这样，格兰特小姐，”他说，“我们现在将带您去那里，如果您不介意的话。之后，我们还需要问您一些问题。”

当她关掉音乐、穿上外套时，她的脸色苍白。但是上汽车时，她相当平静。她真的能够像她表现的那样平静吗？

## 第37页

他们进楼时，埃利奥特仔细地看了看她。她仍然没有流露出丝毫强烈的情感。只是当尸体被推出来、塑料单被揭开的时候，她的手开始发抖了。当然，头部仍然盖着。如果她看不到脸就不能确定的话，他们就得靠指纹和牙医记录了。但是他认为没有必要到这一步。任何认识这位男士的人都会认出他那修长的手指。她迅速地看了一眼尸体，然后向埃利奥特点了点头。

“您确定？”他不得不问。

她摸了一会儿那个人的右手，然后她开始哭了起来。

他们开车回格林尼治的路上没有人说话。阳光仍然灿烂，很多人都把外套搭在胳膊上，这在十一月来说是不常有的。

灰色的天空应该更应景，埃利奥特想，也更配阿曼达·格兰特眼睛里的悲伤。她眼睛直视着前方，明显没有注意到天气，也没有注意到埃利奥特转过头去看她时的那张脸。

## 第 7 章　不轻松的关系

### 第38页

当他们进入阿曼达·格兰特的房子时，那只猫从椅子上跳了下来。它出了房间，鲍恩跟着它去找厨房。自从入了警察这行，他已经习惯于在陌生人的房子里泡茶了。他发现大部分人在喝了一杯很甜的浓茶之后会感觉更好些。

阿曼达·格兰特接过茶，悄声地谢了他。她尝了一口，因为太甜，做了个鬼脸，但是她什么也没说就喝下去了。

当埃利奥特开始提问的时候，她看上去又相当平静了。

“我是一名记者，督察先生，”她说，“我在《世界女性》杂志社工作。我猜您没听说过它吧。”

可是他听说过。萨莉已经开始买这本杂志了，并且他偶尔会看，努力想要了解这杂志哪里吸引她。突然，他记起来他在哪里看到过阿曼达·格兰特的脸，就在每个月的杂志内页第一页。他注意到这张面孔是因为它比那上面其他三张面孔要年轻得多。很明显，她是一位非常成功的女士。

## 第39页

“恐怕我没有时间看杂志，格兰特小姐，”他回答道，并没有全说实话，“您认识福尔利先生很久了吗？”

“差不多四年了，”她说，“我们是在 12 月 31 号，一次新年前夕的派对上遇见的。从那以后我们就开始相当频繁地见面了。”

“有多频繁？”埃利奥特问。

“哦，一个星期见几次，”她回答道，“但是最近没那么频繁了。”她把脸扭到一边。“我的新工作占用了我很多时间，所以他想让我放弃工作。因为这件事我们吵了很多次。上一次我见到他时我们又吵了一架。”

她用一只手捂住双眼。

“那是什么时候的事，格兰特小姐？”埃利奥特问道。

“星期天晚上，”她说，“然后我就去了爱丁堡，昨天下午才回来。这周我本应该打电话的，但是我生他的气，我猜他也有同样的感受。我昨天回来的时候打了电话，但是他不在家。”她的嗓音似乎变了一点点。“那是星期五，”她说，“所以我猜想他比平时更早去见凯瑟琳·克劳瑟了。”

## 第40页

“但是我理解的是他去见的是克劳瑟夫妇二人。”埃利奥特说，听上去比他的本意略微尖刻了些。

“那是罗纳德·克劳瑟愿意这么想，”她回答道，“在亚历克斯妈妈去世后，他对亚历克斯非常好。亚历克斯在世上很孤单，他一开始也需要罗纳德的帮助。但是后来他心情好多了，并且他的生活也有了改变。他不再那么需要罗纳德了，但是罗纳德开始依赖他了。罗纳德相当孤独，他没有太多朋友。”

埃利奥特表现得很感兴趣，但是什么都没说。

“亚历克斯开始发现罗纳德相当无趣，”她继续说，“尽管他从不表现出来。他不愿意伤害别人的感情，而且他不能忘记一直以来罗纳德对他有多好。然而亚历克斯与凯瑟琳有着更多的共同兴趣。他们很喜欢对方，而罗纳德似乎从来不嫉妒。罗纳德对体育感兴趣，可亚历克斯并不感兴趣。但是他以前总是装成感兴趣的样子来让这位老人高兴。”

“您嫉妒吗，格兰特小姐？”埃利奥特想问问，但是现在不是问这个问题的好时候。于是乎，他若有所思地看着她桌上的一张照片。上面是一个金发的瘦高男人，一双黑眼睛正笑盈盈地看着镜头。很帅的小伙子。如果这位是亚历克斯，那么他被众女子所爱就一点儿也不意外了。

## 第41页

她顺着他的视线看过去，然后点了点头，这是这天当中她第二次点头。

“是的，那是亚历克斯。”她说。

“您介意我们借用一下这张照片吗？”埃利奥特问道。

她默默地把照片递给了他。

“关于福尔利先生您还有没有更多的事情想告诉我们呢？”埃利奥特问，“有没有不寻常的事或者不一样的事？”

“嗯，最近他说他总是感觉身体虚弱，而且后来他开始头疼，”她回答道，“在那之前，他从来没有正经生过病。他直到今年才有了一位自己的家庭医生。我想这就是为什么他之前那么担心他的头痛。还有他花了很多时间来思虑他的健康状况。亚历克斯有很多钱，督察先生，而且他几乎不需要工作。他懈怠得起。有些人可能说那是幸运，但是像那样过日子我会不开心。”

有那么一刻她看起来有些不耐烦。然后她继续说：“总之，由于某些原因，他有了一个想法，就是觉得自己的健康出了严重的问题。但是他并不肯说自己认为是什么病。他甚至几周以前在医院做了几项身体检查。”

## 第42页

“检查结果怎么样？”埃利奥特说。

“我不知道，”她回答道，“上次我见到他的时候，结果还没有出来。我一直告诉他那是一个好的预兆。如果他们发现了什么严重的情况，他们立刻就会告诉他的。”

“您得等些日子才能获知全部情况，”埃利奥特说着就想到了病理学家的报告，“干活儿的人越来越少，而工作越来越多。那么，我们需要他的家庭医生的名字和地址。您知道吗？”

“菲利普·维尔弗，”她说，“亚历克斯认识他很多年了。他在布莱克希思工作，所以当亚历克斯需要找医生时，他显然是最合适的选择。他住在新十字区佩皮斯路 54 号。”

“他工作的地方够远的。”埃利奥特说着就想到了昨晚的交通拥堵。

“他买不起布莱克希思的房子。他刚当医生不久。他家很穷，和我家一样。我们两个都得为我们想要的东西去打拼。和亚历克斯不一样。”

她看了看曾经放过福尔利照片的地方，然后垂下了视线。埃利奥特真想把照片还给她。

第43页

“格兰特小姐，”埃利奥特轻声说，“您能想到有什么理由可能会让福尔利先生想要自杀吗？”

她面无血色。她无助地看着埃利奥特，摇了摇头。

“您需要我们替您打电话叫一位朋友来吗？”埃利奥特问道，“他们可以过来陪您坐一会儿。我们等到他们来了再走。”

“谢谢，督察先生，”她说道，“不过我一个人没问题。”

埃利奥特和鲍恩说了再见，但是她似乎没有听到他们说话。埃利奥特心想她是否意识到自己仍然穿着外套。

## 第 8 章　布莱克希思的篝火

第44页

两个男人受到阿曼达·格兰特悲伤情绪的影响，沉默了很长一段时间。直到开到了布莱克希思山顶，埃利奥特才想起今天是盖伊·福克斯之夜。今天草地上没有孩子玩耍，草地周围反而圈起了围栏，还贴着告示，让人们待在围栏外面。围栏里很多工作正在进行。

几组人在研究着几张纸上的东西，并且大喊着指令。工人们正在搬运各种形状和尺寸的烟花，并把它们堆在地上的塑料布上面。在正中间，四个男人正在搭建一个巨大的篝火木堆。

“我觉得福尔利是昨天死的算我们走运，幸好不是今天，”埃利奥特最后说，“今晚的交通状况会是有史以来最糟糕的。”

“长官，您怎么看她？”鲍恩问道，“刚开始，她看起来是那么冷冰冰，像是那些凌厉的职业女性中的一员。”

## 第45页

“我喜欢她，”埃利奥特说，“她不轻易表露自己的感受，但这并不意味着她没有感情。我认为她对福尔利感情很深，尽管他们的关系很明显有问题。”

“她没怎么提到凯瑟琳·克劳瑟，对吧？”鲍恩说，“我很想知道这两个女人对彼此的真正看法是什么。”

福尔利的房子在日光中看起来更招人喜欢了。房子的大小和形状都很完美，而且阳光给那古旧的墙面以更丰富的色泽。尽管是十一月了，玫瑰仍然很漂亮。仿佛这里不可能在前一天发生过可怕的事情。

电话在紧挨大厅木楼梯的一张古董桌子上。电话答录机里有三条信息，有两条是前一天留下的。阿曼达·格兰特 3 点 45 分打了电话说她回来了。几分钟后有个叫菲利普的人邀请福尔利和阿曼达星期天共进午餐。然后是当天早上八点钟，阿曼达·格兰特又打来电话。

“菲利普是阿曼达·格兰特跟我们讲到的那个医生的名字，”埃利奥特记起来了，“我想知道是不是同一个人。”

鲍恩和埃利奥特搜查完这幢房子的时候，时间差不多一点半了。很明显福尔利是一个非常爱整洁的人，所有的物品看起来都各在其位。他们拿走了一本日记、一本地址簿，还有 2200 英镑的现金，这些钱就在他的写字桌上。

## 第46页

“没有人想偷他的钱，”鲍恩说，“所以这不是他被杀的原因。人们怎么会在家里放这么多现金？这么多钱只会招来犯罪分子。”

“哦，他大概认为布莱克希思很安全，”埃利奥特回答道，“记得克劳瑟说过的话吗？像那样的人不相信犯罪会发生在他们身上。我们最好现在去拜访他们一下。我想多了解些她提到的那把枪的事情。”

然而克劳瑟夫妇没在家，于是埃利奥特和鲍恩决定在布莱克希思边上的一家老酒馆里吃午饭。透过窗户，他们能看到工人们正在为晚上的烟花表演做准备。

现在篝火木堆更大了。成群结队的人站着看平放在篝火旁边的盖伊·福克斯模型。在埃利奥特看来，那玩意儿有着黑色的头发和胡须，还穿戴着17世纪的帽子和外套，看起来跟活的差不多。

今晚，很多人会来看它在篝火顶端燃烧。但是很少有人想到那个真实的盖伊·福克斯，他因为试图炸掉议会大厦而被执行火刑。他那么做是出于宗教信仰，而今晚观看的人们大部分对宗教不感兴趣。现如今还有什么重要到让人通过杀戮来捍卫吗？埃利奥特的头脑中浮现出了米基和萨莉的脸。

### 第47页

他想起他得给他们打电话了，但是此刻唯一的电话在酒吧里最吵闹的地方。他叹了口气。还是等等再打电话吧，不过他午饭后可以直接去看看这里的房价。

## 第9章　秘密和谎言

### 第48页

鲍恩按了两次门铃，凯瑟琳·克劳瑟才开了门。埃利奥特再一次讶异于她的魅力。她穿着一件绿色的套衫，颜色和她的眼睛很配。而她脸上流露出的忧伤却让她显得愈加美丽。

罗纳德·克劳瑟正在起居室里读报纸。当他们进来时，他抬起视线，但是埃利奥特还是注意到了刚才他的眼睛正盯着头版的顶端。他明显是刚刚把报纸拿起来。

他看起来在生气，并且他妻子看起来很紧张，但是他们两个都在尽力掩饰。大概在门铃响之前他们正在争吵。埃利奥特决定在不同的房间里分别问他们问题，看看他们的讲述是否一致是很有趣的事。

"我想再问二位几个问题，"他说，"克劳瑟太太，您能带我看看您昨天画画儿的地方吗？刑侦警员鲍恩会在楼下和克劳瑟先生谈话。"

## 第49页

他知道其实鲍恩更愿意和凯瑟琳·克劳瑟谈话，但是这个年轻人并没有把失望表现在脸上。他拿出了笔记本，凯瑟琳·克劳瑟带着埃利奥特离开了。

她带他上了楼，来到一间白色墙面、没有家具的房间，房间里有股好闻的颜料气味。埃利奥特可以看到几幅靠着墙的油画的背面，窗边还有一幅没有画完的。画面的色彩令人惊讶。不像楼下的那些满是蓝色和绿色的画儿，这一幅画儿是用黑色、暗红色和橙色来画的，蕴含着强烈的暴力感。埃利奥特几乎无法相信它是同一个人画的。

"是什么使她变成这种画风的？"他心想，"还有这种改变是何时发生的？我想看看那边的那些画儿是什么样子的。"

他望向窗外，很清楚地看到警员德鲁伊特正站在福尔利家前门外，手里有一支烟。

如果凯瑟琳·克劳瑟经常在这里画画儿的话，她会知道福尔利的一切私生活。

“昨天您在这上面待了多久？”他问道。

“上午的大部分时间，”她说道，“我想我是大概九点半的时候开始画画儿的。我大约十二点歇下来，然后刚过了三点又开始画，我昨天跟您说过。但是我下午没有看到任何来访者。”

## 第49页

“那上午呢？”埃利奥特问。

“嗯，有人确实在我停笔之前来过，”她说，“但是我没有看到他的脸。他从前门进去时我正好抬头看了一眼。”

“所以您不知道他是谁？”埃利奥特问道。

“嗯，”她停顿了一下，“从背后看他有点儿像菲利普·维尔弗。他是亚历克斯的一位朋友，也是他的医生。那个人头发的颜色和菲利普一样，身上的深蓝色外套也像菲利普的。但是我无法确定就是他，督察先生。我只看到他一秒钟。”

“这很有用，”埃利奥特说，“您觉得您丈夫看到他了吗？”

“罗纳德一上午都在后花园干活儿，”她说，“他应该什么也没看见。不过如果他们到外面来，到亚历克斯的花园，我猜他可能会听到点儿什么。您最好问一下他。”

“我们会问的，”埃利奥特回答道，“现在，我们还需要再了解一些福尔利先生的事情。他是什么样的人？”

她直视远方，眼睛里充满泪水。

“一个非常有趣的人，”她说，“也是一个非常善良的人。有时候太善良了。他极不喜欢伤害他人，这点让他相当软弱。”

## 第51页

她似乎对自己这样说感到很抱歉，于是很快继续道：“很难相信有人会想要去伤害他。”

“您昨天说您不相信那是自杀，”埃利奥特说，“什么让您那么确定？”

她迅速看向别处。“我不知道昨天我说了什么了，督察先生。当然，他有可能是自杀。如果处境太艰难了，任何人都可能自杀。”

“那么福尔利先生处境艰难吗？”埃利奥特饶有兴趣地问道。在此之前，他一直以为亚历克斯的生活很轻松。太轻松了，如果阿曼达说的是真的。

“嗯，我能看出他心里有些不愿意谈论的事，”她说，“不过他总是会把他所有的事情都告诉我的。他不对我保密。”

“她说起他就像是在说起爱人。”埃利奥特想。

“别误会，督察先生，”她马上说，“我和亚历克斯关系很密切。他可能是我最好的朋友，但是我们没有私情。我丈夫不担心我们的关系。他知道我们之间发生的一切。”

## 第52页

“我明白了，”埃利奥特说，他根本不相信这番话，“那么，您昨晚提到了一把枪。关于这个您能多说一些吗？”

“我说过吗？”她说着看向别处，“昨天我被吓到了，我忘记我说过什么了。但是我确实记得最近罗纳德和亚历克斯开过一个关于枪的玩笑。那是在亚历克斯为自己的房子买了一幅珍贵的油画之后，罗纳德问他是否想到过会被抢劫，然后亚历克斯说他最好出去买一把枪。可能我昨晚是在想那件事。但他们两个人都不是认真的，督察先生。布莱克希思从没有出过事。”

她看上去好像知道埃利奥特不相信她。她不是一个善于撒谎的人。

“还有，我知道福尔利先生一直在担心他的健康问题，”他继续问，“关于这方面您能跟我说说吗？”

“哦，可以，”她迅速说，好像对换个话题感到很高兴，“他总头痛，并且他把这个很当回事。他母亲的病开始时症状就是头痛，督察先生。她死于脑瘤，您知道，那种病让人很难受。亚历克斯真的越来越忧虑。”

“另外，您会觉得福尔利先生是一个懈怠的人吗？”埃利奥特问，他记得阿曼达·格兰特说过。

## 第53页

“根本不是啊，督察先生，”她回答道，“他没有把他的所有时间都用来做生意，如果您是这个意思的话。但是他有很多其他方面的事情要做。亚历克斯爱音乐，爱书籍和油画，而且在这些方面他花了大量的时间。当然有些人觉得那不是正事，因为不赚钱。”

她看着埃利奥特，好像在思索着他是否也属于这类人。

“他和格兰特小姐关系怎么样？”他问道，“您认为他们在一起开心吗？”

她沉默了一会儿。然后她说：“阿曼达就像世上任何一位年轻女子，督察先生。她想成功，她不明白亚历克斯的价值观不一样。她常常不理解他。这引起了他们之间的问题。”

“什么样的问题？”埃利奥特问。

“亚历克斯想和她结婚，但是她拿不定主意。她想让他对他的生意投入更多的兴趣。这点让亚历克斯很不开心。”

她难过地看了亚历克斯一会儿。

"她没有意识到她是多么幸运，"她说，"现在说这个太晚了。太晚了，什么也改变不了了。"

她用一只手挡住眼睛，想藏住她的泪水。

## 第 10 章　重浴爱河

### 第54页

不像很多男人那样，当有女人哭的时候，埃利奥特并没有感到不舒服。在他的工作中，他习惯了这种情况。他仔细地打量着克劳瑟太太，但是没有表现出来。她显然不开心，但是同样明显的是她在隐瞒着什么。这可能和福尔利的死亡没有关系。或许福尔利真的死于自杀。但是他仍然想知道隐瞒起来的是什么。

尽管如此，此刻他只能问常规的问题。

"还有一件事情让我感兴趣，"他说，"我们在福尔利先生的家里发现了很多钱。他总是在家里放很大数额的现金吗？"

"我不知道，督察先生，"她吃惊地说，"我不经常谈论钱。"

"是啊，"埃利奥特想，"我猜想当您已经有那么多钱的时候也不必谈钱。"

他们走出了房门。埃利奥特在房间外面的一幅画儿前面停下脚步。这幅和楼下的那些画儿很相似。

### 第55页

"我能问一下这是您画的吗？"他说道。

她点点头，又一次露出惊讶的表情，然后他继续说："这幅画儿跟您现在正在画的那幅很不一样啊。"

"哦，我想尝试一下新的风格。"她轻轻地说。她迅速转向楼梯，但是埃利奥特还是看到她的脸开始发红了。

鲍恩和罗纳德·克劳瑟正在大厅里等着他们。

“如果还有什么我们可以告诉你们的，尽管问吧，”罗纳德·克劳瑟说道，“亚历克斯是个非常好的人。我们愿尽可能提供帮助。”

“哦，还真有一件事情。先生，我知道昨天上午您一直在外面干活儿，”埃利奥特说，“您听到福尔利的花园里有什么声音吗？”

“恐怕我没听到什么，督察先生。”罗纳德·克劳瑟说。

他打开门送他们出去，然后站在门口一直看着他们沿着门前小径向大门走去。

他们在车上对比了克劳瑟夫妇的讲述，看起来每一处细节都很吻合。

## 第56页

“长官，那枪的事情呢？”鲍恩问道，“您信吗？”

“一个字都不信，”埃利奥特说道，“他们明显在撒谎。我想知道为什么。你怎么看罗纳德·克劳瑟这个人？”

“呃，他不如他的妻子聪明，”鲍恩回答道，“对于福尔利很明显他感到难过，但是没有他的妻子那么难过。我得说他在担心着什么，或许是害怕着什么。”

“我觉得想让像克劳瑟先生那样的人感到害怕不容易，”埃利奥特说，“他似乎不是个很有想象力的男人。”

“从您所说的来看，长官，凯瑟琳·克劳瑟对阿曼达·格兰特的评价不太高啊。”

“是不高，她似乎觉得她比阿曼达更加理解福尔利。”

“您觉得福尔利和凯瑟琳·克劳瑟有婚外情吗，长官？”

“我不知道，”埃利奥特说，“她明显和他关系非常密切，因为他告诉过她他为什么那么担心自己的头疼。连阿曼达好像都不知道原因。”

“那么我们下面的行动是什么？”鲍恩问道。

“嗯，在周一见到病理学家的报告之前，我们不能再向他们询问了，”埃利奥特说，“但是我们明天第一件事是去拜访一下菲利普·维尔弗。我想知道他是不是凯瑟琳·克劳瑟昨天看到的那个男人。我们到处都能听到他的名字。他可能会告诉我们一些事情。”

## 第57页

他们决定顺便去一下位于格林尼治的福尔利的商店，当他们驶入帕克大街时，他们看到络绎不绝的游客正朝河边走去。很多人正在吃冰激凌，尽管现在天气相当冷，而且天色已经开始变暗了。

这是一条长长的街道，两边是高高的漂亮的房子。房子的窗户和门全都是一样的深蓝色，但是到处种着植物——在门前花园里，在窗台花箱里——给这条街增添了色彩和生机。这里仅有两家商店，都是卖古董的。两家店门挨着门，仿佛在众房环伺当中它们需要彼此的陪伴。在较大的那家商店的门楣上方，有用金色字母写成的福尔利的名字。

橱窗里几乎没有什么东西。其中一扇橱窗里放着一张小桌子，上面有一盏漂亮的金属台灯。另一扇橱窗里一个高大的中式罐子立在一块色彩斑斓的波斯地毯上面。

埃利奥特肯定是疯了才会幻想自己能买得起这里的东西。他看到的房价令他震惊。不过他迟早会赚够钱的，即使他不得不一年到头每个周末都工作。

## 第58页

虽然刚刚四点钟，门上的一块指示牌却显示着“闭店”字样。

但是一位年轻女子正坐在店里的桌子旁边。他敲了一次门，她没有起身，他就又更大声地敲了一次。他举起他的警察证件，随后她马上来到门边。很明显，她刚刚一直在哭。

“我是琳达·斯科特，”她说，“我是这里的经理。我猜您来这儿是为可怜的亚历克斯的事吧。他是个那么好的人。当然，阿曼达打来电话之后，我立刻就把商店关了。您知道事情是怎么发生的吗？”

她已经知道了，埃利奥特就放心了。他不喜欢告诉别人坏消息。不得不把福尔利的死讯告诉人们的差事，他早干够了。

“恐怕现在回答您的问题还为时过早，”他说，“但是您也许会帮到我们。您昨天见过福尔利先生吗？”

“见过。他总是周五来，”她说，“他在这儿大概从 9 点半待到 11 点。”

“他有没有做什么不寻常的事情？”鲍恩问道。

“没有，我认为没有，”她说，“他打了几个电话，还写了几封信。他确实带走了好大一笔钱，但是那不算不寻常。他说他正计划买什么东西。在这一行人们经常更愿意用现金支付，这样可以避税。”

## 第59页

她停了下来，面色慌张。她似乎突然想起她正在和一名警察交谈。

鲍恩微笑着看着她，虽然他通常不觉得人们提到违反法律的事情时有多有趣。

“您知道她拿走了多少钱吗？”鲍恩问道，仍然微笑着。

“就 2000 英镑多点儿，我想，”说着，她翻开了一个大号笔记本，“是的，2200 英镑。”

“走之前再问一件事情，”埃利奥特说，“福尔利先生是一个好老板吗？”

“极好啊，”她说，“他善良而且有人情味儿，非常不同于现如今的大部分雇主。但是最近他一直看起来不开心，似乎在忧虑着什么。他说他总是头痛，但是肯定不只是头痛这件事。”

他们离开商店前，鲍恩记下了她的地址。

“为什么福尔利如此吸引女人？”在车上他问埃利奥特，“她们中没有一个人说他的坏话。这姑娘看起来也快爱上他了。”

### 第60页

“但是这也没给他带来什么好处，对吗？”埃利奥特说，“怎么了，鲍恩？你是在嫉妒他吗？”

他是在开玩笑，但是一看鲍恩的表情，就看出来这位是相当正经的。

“在这个案子结束前不要对琳达·斯科特有任何想法。”埃利奥特警告他。

“不会的，长官。”鲍恩说。

“你要对她保持开放的态度，”埃利奥特继续说，“在这起谋杀中，她可能有犯罪嫌疑。”

他并不是真的有理由要这样想，而且他不得不承认她似乎比鲍恩通常喜欢的那类女孩子要更好一些。但是就凭鲍恩的运气，不会有什么惊喜的。

## 第 11 章　家和家人

### 第61页

他终于到了家。埃利奥特摘下领带，给自己倒了一杯啤酒，然后拨了萨莉父母家的电话号码。他有些希望没有人在家，但是没等电话铃声响第二次，萨莉就接了电话。听到他的声音，她听起来很高兴。

“喂，罗德，”她说，“你一整天都到哪儿去了？我给局里打了四次电话。”

“大部分时间在布莱克希思和格林尼治，”他回答道，“我手上有一起新的谋杀案，但是这个案子我还没有多少进展。死者是一个人见人爱的男人。他的家里放着很多现金，却一点儿没有被偷。有可能是自杀，但是我们要到星期一才能知道。你一切都好吗？”

“是的，我们今天过得很开心，”她说，“你还得待在伦敦，真是太遗憾了。但是你现在听起来比星期五开心多了。”

“是的，很抱歉我那时情绪那么不好，”埃利奥特说，“米基怎么样？”

## 第62页

“玩儿得很开心。但是他很想你，他不停地提到你。你最好跟他说说话。”

“喂，爸爸。”米基说道。

埃利奥特笑着听他儿子说着沙滩和今晚的烟花表演的事情。他总是从生活中得到那么多乐趣。没有和他在一起，埃利奥特感到很愧疚。

但是当他放下电话的时候，他意识到他累了。在电视前度过一个安静夜晚的想法突然看起来很不错。《今日赛事》这个节目对于今晚来说就足以令人激动了，如果他能足够长时间保持清醒来看节目的话。

他很高兴萨莉不和他生气了。实际上，她从来不会生很长时间的气。但是这样也不能免除埃利奥特在争吵之后的不安感，万事总有第一次。

他给自己做了点儿吃的，进了起居室，然后打开了新闻。政府又陷入麻烦中了。埃利奥特努力在室外的烟花爆炸声中听清详细内容。但是他太累了，提不起兴趣来。

周六晚上的医院情景剧看到一半，他就睡着了，但是两个小时后足球粉丝的大喊声唤醒了他。西汉姆刚刚进了一个决胜球，离球赛结束还有三分钟。埃利奥特笑着关了电视。

## 第63页

第二天早上天气变了。这是入冬的第一天。

他到办公室的时候，鲍恩已经在那儿了。埃利奥特觉得他几个月都没有这会儿看起来那么开心。

“早，鲍恩。你昨晚过得好吗？”他问。

“嗯，我认为福尔利的日记可能会帮到我们，长官，”他说道，“所以我把它带回家看了一下。他明显不想让其他人看懂。日记是用希腊语和拉丁语混合在一起写的，但是我觉得我正开始弄懂它是怎么写成的了。不过，我还是需要花点儿时间才能读懂。”

“教育真是绝妙的东西。”埃利奥特说。不过他自己中学毕业就当了警察。当时他并没有觉得大学教育会对他有多大帮助。阅读对于他来说从来不重要，他更喜欢从经验中学习。

但是他对这个年轻的小伙子很满意。鲍恩一直是个工作麻利的警察，并且现在他对这个案子还有了额外的兴趣。他们越快结案，他就可以越快找琳达·斯科特碰一下他的桃花运。埃利奥特希望他对于她的感情不要影响他的判断。

## 第64页

“那么，我们最好去拜访一下菲利普·维尔弗，”埃利奥特说，“但愿他在家里。”

“星期天的早上大部分人都会在家，”鲍恩说，“除了警察。”

佩皮斯路是一条美丽的街道，离埃利奥特家很近。这条街上的房屋高大，里面房间大，天花板也高。很多房子都被分隔成了公寓，但是54号仍然是一栋独家居住的房子。冬天的晚上，埃利奥特有时候透过亮晃晃的窗户能看到屋子里面。漂亮的壁炉和壁炉上方墙上的大镜子让这所房子看上去总是那么吸引人。

埃利奥特看着屋前花园里玫瑰的颜色快变成棕色了，有点儿难过，大概是因为昨夜寒冷的天气，他想。这些花儿很快就要死了。他知道等他有时间去看自己的花园时，他也会看到同样的景象。

鲍恩按门铃的当口，埃利奥特边向自己的双手呵着气来保持温暖，边透过窗户往里面看。一个男人和一个小男孩儿正一起坐在沙发上，他们在看一本图画书。看到没有人点燃壁炉里的火，埃利奥特很失望。

## 第65页

一个高个儿的黑发女子打开了门，她的手里拿着一支烟。她看起来脸色苍白而且焦虑不安。她盯着他们看了几秒钟却没有说话，就好像她没有看到他们。

“什么事？”她还是开口了。

“我们想找菲利普·维尔弗谈谈，”埃利奥特介绍了他们自己以后说道，“他在家吗？”

她走进去并且喊着：“菲利普！警察来了。”

几秒钟之后，坐在沙发上的那个男人出现了。他高高的，很英俊，留着深色短发，戴着眼镜。和他的妻子一样，他显得紧张不安，但是他似乎更能控制住。那个小男孩儿和他在一起，紧紧抱住他的大腿，睁大眼睛盯着警察。埃利奥特想他应该是五岁左右。

“我是菲利普·维尔弗，”这个男人说，“抱歉，我妻子让你们在外面久等了。请进来吧。”

他们进了那间埃利奥特从外面看到的房间。屋里出奇地凌乱。报纸和杂志散落在地板上，旁边是几只没有洗的杯子和装满了烟头的烟灰缸。即使这样也不能遮掩一个事实，那就是这是一个漂亮的房间。

“抱歉，屋里太乱，”维尔弗说，“昨天早上有朋友过来，并且给我们带来了噩耗。我们的一位朋友突然去世了。”

## 第66页

他难过地看着他们。

“我猜想这也是你们来的原因吧。”他说。

“恐怕是这样的，先生。”埃利奥特说。

维尔弗把他的手搭在小男孩儿的肩上。

“去找你妈妈，萨姆，”他说，“她在里屋。”

孩子慢慢站起来，然后出去了，什么话都没有说。

“他在为亚历克斯的事难过，”他爸爸说，“亚历克斯对小孩子很和善，萨姆真心喜欢他。你们弄清楚他发生什么事了吗，督察先生？”

“还没有，先生，”埃利奥特说，“但是我们正指望着您也许能帮我们。我们知道您非常了解他。您也是他的家庭医生，是吗？”

“才当了几个月，督察先生，”维尔弗说，“以朋友的身份我更了解他。”

“我们听说他病了，”埃利奥特说，“这是真的吗？”

“算不上，”维尔弗回答道，“尽管他一度是这么想的。他最近常常头疼，他觉得可能很严重，但是我知道并不严重。他甚至说服了我给他在盖伊医院安排做一些检查，完全是浪费钱。但是为了不让他担心，我也只能做这些了。”

### 第68页

“您预计结果什么时候出来？”埃利奥特问。

“哦，这个星期已经出来了。当然是没事。他大概只是需要配一副新眼镜。”

他再次扭过头去。“可怜的亚历克斯。”他说。

## 第 12 章　一种婚姻

### 第69页

有几秒钟没人说话。他们能听到隔壁房间里维尔弗的妻子在和孩子说话，她听起来在生气，小男孩儿好像什么都没有说。

“对不起，督察先生，”维尔弗说，“我最好去把萨姆带过来。这阵子莉萨觉得孩子很难哄，亚历克斯的离世对她影响很大。对我们家的人影响都很大。”

他出去了一会儿，然后带着儿子回来了。小男孩儿正在哭，他的头深埋在他爸爸的肩头。

“好了，萨姆，”维尔弗温柔地说，“妈妈这会儿只是有点儿忙。”

“她总是很忙，”萨姆说，“她从来不和我玩儿。”

“我一会儿就带你去公园，”他的爸爸说，“我们要去踢足球。但是我必须先和这些人说会儿话。上楼去准备好，萨姆。我想我今天早上在你的卧室看到过足球。”

## 第70页

小男孩儿不哭了，并向门口走去。

“我们会尽快，先生，”埃利奥特说，“那么，您认识福尔利先生多久了？”

“从大学开始，”维尔弗说，“我们第一天见面就发现我们有很多共同点。我们都是在很小的时候父母一方就去世了，这点好像把我们带到了一起。并且当我遇到莉萨时，她也喜欢他。那很重要。督察先生，您结婚了吗？”

埃利奥特说结了。

“那您会懂得那是什么感觉，”维尔弗继续道，“亚历克斯家里有钱，像莉萨一样，并且那对她很重要。她似乎不喜欢我的其他朋友，所以后来我都不和他们见面了。当我开始学医时，莉萨很不高兴。我不得不非常努力，而她也不经常来见我。我不能指望她在她不喜欢的人身上花时间。您明白那是怎么一回事，督察先生。”

“当然。”埃利奥特说。但是实际上他不明白那种关系。萨莉和他总是接受彼此的朋友。

“那么您最后一次见到福尔利先生是什么时候？”他问道。

“星期五，”维尔弗说，“当我打电话说给他送检查结果的时候，他让我第二天过去。他说他想要听听我对于某事的建议。所以我12点左右去了他家。但是当我到那儿的时候，他又改主意了。他说要商量的那件事不再重要了，虽然他看上去对什么事情有些担心。我只待了简单喝杯咖啡那么长的时间，然后我就回诊所开午餐会议去了。”

## 第71页

“您记得您是什么时间离开的吗，先生？”鲍恩问道。

“大约 12 点 20 分，”维尔弗说，“但是在那之后我还是忍不住担心他。过了一会儿我打电话约他一起吃午饭，但是他不在家。我在他的电话答录机里留了一条口信。我想你们已经听到了。”

他的脸色变了。

“那时候他已经死了吗，督察先生？”他问道。

“恐怕我们还不知道，”埃利奥特回答道，“维尔弗医生，您在那里的时候福尔利先生正在喝酒吗？”

“酒？”维尔弗问道，“没有。亚历克斯不怎么喝酒，并且他肯定不会一个人喝酒。”

“谢谢您，先生，”埃利奥特说，“现在，只有一件事情我还想问您。福尔利先生是个什么样的人？”

## 第72页

维尔弗看了他一会儿。

“要描述一个很熟悉的人是很难的，”他说，“但我会试试。他很容易沟通。你什么都可以跟他说，然后他总会给出正确的意见。他总是很严肃，但是他也可以很有趣。我会非常想念他的。”

“那您会觉得他是个脆弱的人吗，先生？”埃利奥特问道，他想起凯瑟琳·克劳瑟说过的话。

医生没有马上回答。他看着壁炉，似乎沉思了一会儿。

“他和我们大家没什么两样，督察先生。”最后他说。

萨姆抱着一个足球走进来的时候，他突然笑了一下。小男孩儿看了看埃利奥特，然后坐在了地毯上。

就在他们离开之前，埃利奥特问道："先生，顺便问一下，您能想到某个可能想伤害福尔利先生的人吗？"

"想不到，"维尔弗说，"大家都爱亚历克斯。"

他关了前门。透过窗户，埃利奥特看到萨姆坐在地板上，耐心地等待他的爸爸。他记不起米基在那个年纪有过坐得如此安静的时候。有那么一刻他为那个孩子感到担心。他过着怎样的家庭生活呢？

## 第73页

"你觉得他这个人怎么样？"他们一上车，埃利奥特就问。

"嗯，很明显他爱他的儿子，"鲍恩说道，"但是我可不喜欢处于他的处境，我可不想跟那样一个妻子生活。她长得够漂亮，但是显然她在控制着他的生活，而且她好像也没有花多少时间在孩子身上。"

"但是他肯定比他表面上要更强势，"埃利奥特说，"他妻子没能阻止他成为一名医生。而且在培训期间结婚可不是件容易的事。当然，你能看出来为什么她不喜欢他当医生。不仅是因为工作时间长。她太看重钱，而新入行的医生不会挣很多钱的。"

他看了鲍恩一会儿。

"这对你来说也是一个经验，"他说道，"谨慎对待你选择的女人。而且如果她们不能让你开心，就不要和她们在一起了。"

鲍恩看起来有点儿尴尬，埃利奥特就换了话题。

"福尔利肯定是个万人迷，"他说，"还不单单受女人欢迎呢。但是我想知道的是当我问到福尔利是不是个脆弱的人时，维尔弗在想什么。"

"就是，"鲍恩说，"他也在对我们隐瞒着什么。"

### 第74页

“好了，至少现在我们知道星期五拜访福尔利的人就是维尔弗，”埃利奥特说，“并且我们知道了福尔利不是真生病了，这就消除了一种可能自杀的原因。那还有什么其他事情令他忧心忡忡呢？”

“而且如果他从来不一个人喝酒的话，为什么他当时在喝酒呢？”鲍恩问道，“可能某个人在维尔弗离开之后来看了他。可能是要卖给他东西的人。那可能就是他的房间里有那么多钱的原因。可能那个人谋杀了他，然后清洗了第二只酒杯。”

“有可能，”埃利奥特说，“但是谁想谋杀他呢？大家好像都很喜欢他。我们得再去和邻居谈谈，看是否有人看到了什么。你能安排一下吗？而且你最好带阿曼达·格兰特来他的房子看看。虽然那里看起来不像丢了什么东西，但是我们应该确定一下。我有一种感觉，这个案子不会像我最初想得那么简单。”

## 第 13 章　终于到家了

### 第75页

埃利奥特坐在他的电脑旁，看着他星期五开始起草的一份报告。可是他脑子里满是关于福尔利这个案子的疑问，无法将它们抛在一边。

为什么克劳瑟夫妇不跟他说实话呢？凯瑟琳·克劳瑟和福尔利有私情吗？是什么让她突然改变了她的绘画风格？星期五维尔弗离开后有人去拜访过福尔利吗？如果有人在一点以后到福尔利家，然后从后门出去的话，凯瑟琳·克劳瑟就不会看到那人。还有，福尔利为了什么而忧心忡忡呢？

埃利奥特很努力地工作。他还有另外三份报告要写，而且这些全都本该在几天前就写完。但是他忍不住去思考这个案子。到他回家的时候，他还是几乎什么都没写。

“爸爸！”他一进门米基就叫他，“昨晚您看到那个精彩的进球了吗？”

“在《今日赛事》里那个？”埃利奥特问道，“那个时候你还没有上床睡觉吗？”

## 第76页

“妈妈说我可以熬夜看比赛的。”米基说。

“他的眼睛几乎都睁不开了。”萨莉说。

“我也一样。”埃利奥特说。他各亲了他们两个一下。

萨莉已经开始做晚餐了。埃利奥特很少下厨，除了星期天的午餐和每个星期三萨莉晚下班的那顿。她在路易斯汉姆学院做兼职教师，通常她下了课刚好可以去接三点半放学的米基，在其他日子里则由她的妹妹照顾米基。

他刚在餐桌旁坐下，就放松下来了。福尔利的死是一个让他惦记的问题，但是不会再让他烦恼了。福尔利没有孩子，也没有自己的家人了。当然，他的朋友会想念他，但是他们有各自的生活。并且阿曼达·格兰特也足够坚强去重新开始。就算克劳瑟夫妇和维尔弗夫妇的婚姻出了问题，也不关埃利奥特的事。他希望病理学家会说这是自杀，然后这个案件就结了。

但是埃利奥特的感觉告诉他这个案子要比自杀复杂，而且从警十八年，他相信自己的感觉。他知道有两个人在撒谎，或许更多。他们在尽力遮掩什么呢？

## 第77页

然而，所有的一切都将等到明天。现在该是他听米基说话的时间了。他微笑着听儿子开始给他讲昨晚的烟花表演。

# 第 14 章　但这是谋杀吗？

## 第78页

通常来讲，如果埃利奥特周末一直工作的话，他就会觉得星期一早上特别不愉快。但是他今天醒来的时候心情很愉快，这种心情一直持续到他到达警察局为止。

鲍恩又一次在他之前到达了。他说他已经到了半个小时了。

“你怎么了？”埃利奥特问道，“上个星期你几乎没有准时到过。肯定是恋爱了。”

鲍恩真希望埃利奥特别提他的私生活了。

“我就是对这个案子感兴趣，”鲍恩难为情地回答道，“而且今天有很多事情要做。顺便说一下，阿曼达·格兰特没有发现福尔利的房子里丢了什么东西。”

“如我所料啊，”埃利奥特说，“我们拿到报告了没有？”

“拿到了，长官。病理学家刚到，”鲍恩回答道，“他们好像一大早就开工了。我们得到了关于那把枪的报告。它是一把二战时的军用枪。现在这种枪不常见了，它几乎算是一件收藏品了。当然，没有任何关于这把枪的记录。”

## 第79页

“这真遗憾，”埃利奥特说，“看来不会有什么机会找出它的来源了。它很有可能被藏在某个人的车库里很多年了。”

埃利奥特从咖啡机那儿取了一杯咖啡，然后坐下来读病理学家的报告。

“让我们期待这份报告能告诉我们一些更有用的东西吧，”他说道，“他是不是自杀呢？这是我们需要知道的。”

但是他的希望落空了。报告上说死者是在下午 3 点 15 分到 3 点 45 分之间被子弹击中头部而死的，开枪者可能是他本人，也可能是他人。死的时候，枪抵着额头，然后一击毙命。无暴力迹象。死者生前身体非常健康，但是在他的胃里和血液里有大量酒精。

“那么，它看起来不像一场意外，”埃利奥特说，“一个人要不是想自杀，是不会坐在一把舒服的椅子上，拿着一把枪指着自己的头的。但是谁开的枪呢？鲍恩，你怎么想？这是谋杀还是自杀？”

## 第80页

“有太多的人在对我们隐瞒实情，”鲍恩说，“我不相信这是一起简单的自杀案。虽然明显有人想让我们认为是这样。”

“自杀案就简单吗？”埃利奥特问道，“但是我认为你说得对。现在我们多少算是知道他什么时间死的了。那么凯瑟琳·克劳瑟在三点半听到的声音很可能就是枪声，如果她告诉我们的是真话的话。去查查那段时间谁有不在场证明，鲍恩。我们还得去收集指纹。我们需要看看是否他们中某些人的指纹跟我们在福尔利家里找到的指纹相吻合。”

“好的，长官，”鲍恩说，“并且福尔利似乎喝了好多酒，远不止一杯酒。”

“所以说嘛，你可能是对的，鲍恩，”埃利奥特说，“可能福尔利那天确实邀请了某人去吃午饭。邻居们都说了些什么？”

“没有什么重要的东西。没人看到有什么情况。”

“又或许福尔利喝酒是为了让自杀更容易一些，”埃利奥特若有所思地继续说道，“所有人都一直提到他在担忧着什么事情。你在他的日记里发现什么有用的东西了吗？”

“还没有，”鲍恩说，“读得很费劲。我已经好久没有读拉丁文和希腊文了。但是我会继续努力的。”

### 第81页

埃利奥特坐在他的办公桌旁，昨天留下的活儿还瞪着眼看着他，他希望在鲍恩回来之前能完成他所有的报告。他叹了一口气。现如今刑警也得写很多东西。这工作并不是一直这样的。

埃利奥特一直忙过了午餐时间，就在两点半刚过，他终于完成了最后一份报告。他穿上外套，然后穿过马路去了女王之首酒吧。他刚一进门，酒吧招待员就动手给他倒了一杯啤酒。

酒吧这会儿没什么人，除了吧台的一头有一堆闹哄哄的学生。他们都喝完了酒水，但是好像并不急着离开。

埃利奥特坐到窗边，尽可能远离他们。啤酒口味不错。他翻开报纸，然后翻到体育版，决定让自己休息上半个小时。写了那么多东西，他理所应当要歇一会儿了。

但是他才刚刚看了星期六西汉姆比赛报道的开头，鲍恩就从门口走进来了。埃利奥特叹了口气，但是鲍恩带来的消息赶走了他脑子里所有关于足球的念头。

# 第 15 章　揭露谎言

## 第82页

“抱歉了，长官，”鲍恩说，“但是我觉得您会很想尽早听到这件事。福尔利好像有个清洁工，叫布鲁克太太。她今天早上去了他家，他们不让她进去，她就恼了。星期一和星期四是她给他打扫卫生的日子，并且她星期三给克劳瑟家打扫卫生。

“不管怎样，她给了我们一些很有趣的信息。福尔利好像在星期三下午去看过凯瑟琳·克劳瑟，当时罗纳德没有在家。”

“这当真是有趣，”埃利奥特说，“克劳瑟太太告诉我们她一个星期都没有见过他了。关于这次串门布鲁克太太说了什么？”

“福尔利貌似在那儿待了大约一个小时，”鲍恩回答道，“起居室的门是关着的，所以她什么也没听到。但是当他们出来的时候，克劳瑟夫人的脸色惨白如纸，并且福尔利看上去也非常难受。”

“我想知道对这件事凯瑟琳·克劳瑟得怎么说。”埃利奥特说。

## 第83页

“但这还不是全部，长官，”鲍恩继续道，“布鲁克太太说克劳瑟有一把旧枪。看样子，以前是他父亲的。有一次他擦枪的时候，她进了那个房间。他迅速把枪放回写字台的一个抽屉里，但没等放进去的时候她已经看到了。她说她每次进到那间起居室，都想知道那把枪是否还在那里。”

“他把枪放在一张写字台里面？”埃利奥特说，“真蠢。而且我认为他没有持枪许可。那么，这值得我们想想。那么指纹呢？有没有什么好运气？”

“嗯，长官，”鲍恩说，“房子里除了福尔利的指纹外，还发现四组新留下的指纹。”

“所以，我们所要做的就是去查明这些指纹是谁的。我们怀疑的对象是克劳瑟夫妇、维尔弗夫妇、阿曼达·格兰特和布鲁克太太。我们能确定他们每个人星期五下午的行踪吗？”

“这个嘛，我们知道布鲁克太太全天都和她的妹妹在一起。而维尔弗从 12 点 45 分到 6 点都在诊所，”鲍恩说，“他开了两个会，后来还给病人看了病，他没有空闲时段。还有，他妻子那天在格林尼治和一个朋友吃午饭，她在 3 点 15 分离开去接她儿子放学。”

## 第84页

“另外三位呢？”埃利奥特问。

“我们还没有核实他们的讲述，”鲍恩说，“凯瑟琳·克劳瑟独自在家。罗纳德在外面散步，但是他不记得看到谁了。阿曼达·格兰特回来的时候就直接回她自己家了。”

“可是还有一些其他的情况，长官，”他继续道，“我在诊所等候的时候又看了几页福尔利的日记，然后我发现了一些很有趣的事情。似乎亚历克斯·福尔利并不是大家认为的那种青年才俊。他有地下情。”

“和凯瑟琳·克劳瑟吗？”埃利奥特问道。

“恐怕我还不能跟您那么说，”鲍恩说，“他把每一个人的名字都改了。”

“那，我想我们最好去看看罗纳德的枪，你觉得呢？”埃利奥特说。

他站起身，留下喝了一半的啤酒。那些学生还坐在吧台的那头。如果酒吧招待员允许的话，他们可能会待上一下午。酒吧里要比他们租的房子暖和得多。

埃利奥特按响克劳瑟家的门铃时，他有些兴奋。所有的线索似乎都要串到一起了。运气好的话，到晚上这个案子就可以结了。

## 第85页

但是克劳瑟夫妇二人都没在家。

“我猜他跟平常一样散步去了，”埃利奥特说，“但是我疑惑的是她会在哪儿呢。我本以为她会在房间里画画儿。”

他抬头看了看窗户。是他的幻觉吗，还是他真的看到有人快速从窗户那儿闪开了？他再次按响了门铃，这次至少按了五秒钟，但还是没有人来应门。

“我们去周六去过的那个酒吧里等等吧，”他说，“至少那里还暖和，而且我可以继续吃我的午饭。”

今天酒吧人少多了，他们很快就找到了一个位子。埃利奥特看向窗外，一时间忘了上个周六是盖伊·福克斯之夜。现在外面既没有围栏也没有烟花，人们像平常一样四处走着，那天的篝火留下的唯一痕迹就是地面上的黑色斑痕。

突然，他看到草地的那头有一个穿着黑色外套的高个子男人。埃利奥特觉得他认出了他。

“我认为那是罗纳德·克劳瑟，”他说，“你看呢，鲍恩？”

## 第86页

而没等鲍恩答话，给埃利奥特端来三明治的酒吧招待员就回答了他的话。

“是的，那是克劳瑟先生，先生，”他说，“这个时候他总是在这里，无论雨天还是晴天。他三点来，四点走，像时钟一样规律。大多数人都觉得在同一片草地上走来走去，也从不跟别人说话，很没意思。但是他似乎不在意。总有奇怪的人。”

“我猜星期五您在这里没有看到他。”埃利奥特说。

“星期五?”酒吧招待员说，“我当然看到了。每天我都能看到他。开始我以为他那天来晚了，但是结果是我的表快了。像我说的，您可以从他的来去判断时间。”

埃利奥特吃完三明治，看到克劳瑟转身回家了。他看了看自己的手表，正好四点钟，酒吧招待员说的是实话。所以在福尔利死亡的时候，克劳瑟还在外面散步。

但是这两位警察还是跟着他回到他家。罗纳德·克劳瑟不会是凶手，但是他和他的妻子还有很多问题要回答。

## 第 16 章　嫉妒

### 第87页

克劳瑟夫妇微笑着打开门，但是埃利奥特没有回以笑容。他知道他们根本不乐意见到他，他们的礼貌和文雅只是一个幌子，从一开始他们就在和他斗心计。

他没做任何铺垫，直接问克劳瑟有没有一把枪。这个男人的脸一下子就白了，他的妻子扑通就坐了下来，好像她的腿失去了所有力气。

“这次我要听实话，”埃利奥特说，“我们已经浪费了够多时间了。”

“好的，督察先生，”克劳瑟说，“我有一把枪，已经好几年了。它是属于我父亲的。他留着它是为了记住那场战争，而且他还留了一颗子弹。他去世的时候，我把枪收藏了起来好纪念父亲。现在看当时那么做真是愚蠢。”

“如果您没有持枪许可的话，那就是犯罪，”埃利奥特说，“我可以看一下吗?”

罗纳德·克劳瑟用双手捂住了脸。

“不在我这里，督察先生。大约三个星期前亚历克斯拿走了。当时我们正在和朋友一起吃晚饭，有人讨论起战争。我喝得相当多，而且愚蠢地跟他们说了这把枪的事。亚历克斯喜欢有年头的东西，所以他当然想看看这把枪。

## 第88页

“然后他说它可能值一大笔钱，他问他是否可以借去估个价。我没有觉得这件事有坏处，于是我就把枪给他了。我告诉他里面有一颗子弹，但是他没放在心上。他说他知道怎么用枪，他在学校的时候学过。”

埃利奥特感到心里直冒火气。这些人觉得他们生活在怎样的世界里面?难道他们觉得自己可以凌驾于法律之上吗?

“那天的晚餐派对上还有谁?”埃利奥特问道。

然而没等答案说出口，他就觉得自己知道了。克劳瑟夫妇、维尔弗夫妇，还有阿曼达·格兰特，这个在福尔利去世之前一直围绕着他的联系紧密的小圈子。

“为什么您之前没有告诉我们这件事?”他问道。

罗纳德·克劳瑟说他本来想说，可是接着他突然意识到持有枪支是违法的，所以他和他妻子就决定最好守口如瓶。

“克劳瑟先生，我们得请您即刻到警察局去，”埃利奥特说，“我们需要知道杀害了福尔利先生的那把枪是不是您的。”

克劳瑟夫妇相互对视，他们似乎很害怕。

## 第89页

“还有，克劳瑟太太，您能告诉我们您最后一次见福尔利是什么时候吗？”

她抬起她碧绿的眼睛，看向埃利奥特的眼睛。

“正如我告诉过您的，督察先生，”她回答道，“是一个星期之前，是在星期五。”

“关于这件事您能仔细想想吗？”埃利奥特说。

“我不需要，”她说，“我记得非常清楚。”

“克劳瑟太太，”埃利奥特说，“我也得请您跟我们去一趟警察局。关于亚历克斯·福尔利的死亡，我们还有问题要问您。”

“我？”她说，“您要审问我？可我以为……”

她突然不说了。罗纳德·克劳瑟闭上了眼睛，他看起来就像是一个正在做噩梦的人。

埃利奥特告诉鲍恩不要让这对夫妻独自待在一起。他不想给他们再编一个故事的机会。

在警察局，他们被带进了不同的房间。当埃利奥特给他们看那把枪的时候，他们都点头确认了。

罗纳德·克劳瑟看起来很疲惫，而且比埃利奥特第一次见到他的时候苍老多了，他的妻子也突然显露出中年的面相。埃利奥特决定首先讯问她。

## 第90页

“有人告诉我们福尔利先生在上个星期三下午去了您家。”他说。

“是吗？我猜想那个人是布鲁克太太吧，”在短暂的沉默之后她回答道，“我完全把她给忘了。”

可能像布鲁克太太那样的人对于她来说无足轻重，不值得记住。

埃利奥特再次纳闷儿亚历克斯·福尔利是哪种人。一个男人怎么能做到与像凯瑟琳·克劳瑟和阿曼达·格兰特这种差别很大的两位女性都保持如此亲密的关系？

“是的，没错，”凯瑟琳·克劳瑟继续说道，“亚历克斯的确在那个时候来看过我。我们讨论了一些非常私密的事情。亚历克斯甚至让我不要告诉罗纳德这件事。”

“出了一件残忍的死亡案件，那就没有什么私密可言了，”埃利奥特不耐烦地说道，“这您应当很清楚。”

她沉默了好一会儿。

“好吧，亚历克斯一直和某人有私情，”她最后说道，“我想您会称它为风流韵事，可是他对于这件事非常不开心。事情开始于一次聚会后的晚上，当时阿曼达不在，他感到孤独落寞。当然，他事后就后悔了，唯愿这件事没有发生。但是那个女人说她爱上他了，而他又不知道如何在不伤害她的情况下结束这段关系。她是他的一位朋友的妻子。这让这件事情很棘手。这也是我之前没有告诉您的原因。”

## 第91页

“她是谁？”埃利奥特问道。

“莉萨·维尔弗。”凯瑟琳·克劳瑟说，面露气愤。

“克劳瑟太太，您爱福尔利先生吗？”埃利奥特问道。

她看了埃利奥特一会儿。

“或许爱吧，”她回答道，“我们是很亲密，但是我们之间是清白的，督察先生。我不会做任何伤害罗纳德的事。他一直对我这么好。”

“当您听到这段婚外情的时候您是什么心情？”

“非常生气。您已经看到我最新的那幅作品了，督察先生。但是那不只是嫉妒。我觉得亚历克斯太傻了。莉萨不是好人，可是他总是相信每个人最好的一面。她的丈夫对她很迷恋，但是她不在乎他，也不在乎她的儿子。她之所以喜欢亚历克斯是因为他有钱。她认为她已经得到他了，所以她也不打算对他放手。亚历克斯心不够硬，结束不了这段关系。当然，还有，他对自己的健康状况忧心忡忡。”

## 第92页

“关于这段婚外情您对他说了什么？”埃利奥特问道。

“我告诉他应该立刻终结这件事，”她回答道，“我也告诉他我觉得他是多么愚蠢。”

“可是您之前为什么没有告诉我们您和福尔利先生最后一次见面的事情呢？”

“哦，我真的不知道，督察先生。我笨死了。”

她真的不是一个善于撒谎的人，埃利奥特又一次这么认为。他感到非常不耐烦。还会有什么原因让她继续撒谎呢？他知道了那把枪，知道了亚历克斯的最后一次来访，也知道了他的私情，而且她甚至都承认了自己的嫉妒。还有什么是她不得不隐瞒的呢？

然后埃利奥特明白了，她肯定是在尽力保护她的丈夫。

“克劳瑟太太，”他说，“我们知道在福尔利先生死亡的时候，您丈夫不在他家附近。”

她盯着埃利奥特，似乎不确定要不要相信他的话。

“他在外面散步时有人看到他了。”他接着说道。

“哦，感谢上帝，”她说，“我一直都提心吊胆的。我以前从不知道罗纳德也会嫉妒，但是他突然开始询问我和亚历克斯之间的关系。他总是禁不住要谈到这个话题。最近亚历克斯没有花很多时间和他在一起，因为亚历克斯在忧虑自己的问题。可是罗纳德以为这和我有关。我不知道罗纳德是更嫉妒亚历克斯还是更嫉妒我，但是这种状况很令人害怕。

## 第93页

“我真的不相信他会杀了亚历克斯。但是他不停地问我在他出去的时候亚历克斯是否来见过我。我不能告诉他星期三亚历克斯来过的事，因为亚历克斯让我保证不告诉别人。但是我认为可能罗纳德看到了他离开我家。反正，罗纳德能看出我对什么事很不高兴。

“我不想在他面前告诉你们亚历克斯来我家的事，这样会让情况变得更糟糕。当然，也没有什么事情可让他嫉妒的。相信我，督察先生，我和亚历克斯之间真的清清白白。”

或许吧，如果精神上的不算，埃利奥特想。

最后，他认为她告诉他的是真话。作为一个强势的女人，她显然不习惯撒谎。但是她由对福尔利的感情而产生的内疚感让她左右为难。这也浪费了他很多时间。

## 第94页

他目送凯瑟琳和罗纳德·克劳瑟一起离开警察局。看得出来，过去的几天里他们一直生活在恐慌当中，两人都相信是对方杀死了福尔利。他想知道他们回家以后会怎样来解释自己的想法。

“可是如果他们俩谁都没有谋杀亚历克斯·福尔利，那他是怎么死的呢？”埃利奥特琢磨着，“我们终于知道了近来让他这么忧心的是什么事，但是他和莉萨·维尔弗的关系肯定不足以让他自杀。

“能肯定的是，我们现在发现了另外两个可能想让他死的人。菲利普·维尔弗，如果他知道他的妻子有婚外情的话。还有莉萨·维尔弗，如果福尔利试图要终结二人的关系的话。但是他们两个人那天下午都和其他人在一起。这是没有疑问的。”

“不。如果星期五下午还有人和福尔利在一起的话，就只有一个人有可能了。”

## 第 17 章　串联线索

### 第95页

当阿曼达·格兰特给埃利奥特和鲍恩开门时，她的表情很惊讶。但是她镇定地让他们进来。她还穿着周六早上穿的那身牛仔裤和毛衣，但是今天她看起来更像一个十多岁的女孩儿，而不是一个成功的记者。

埃利奥特感到非常失望。他第一眼见到她就觉得喜欢她，而且他看人一般都不会这么走眼。她肯定是一个性格刚强、感情浓烈的女人。还有他相信在恰当的情形下，大部分人都可能会杀人。可能她发现了福尔利的风流韵事，而且无法接受。但是他之前认为她是一个勇于承担的人。为什么她没有立即认罪，而是努力掩盖呢？

“格兰特小姐，”他说，“我们想知道您从爱丁堡回来后究竟做了什么。”

“今天早上我告诉刑侦警员鲍恩了，”她用低沉的声音说，“两点零五分飞机在伦敦城市机场着陆。我从停车场取了我的车，然后开车回来。路上花了一个多小时。那天交通状况很糟糕。”

### 第96页

“我理解的是没有人见过您。”埃利奥特继续说。

“没有，”她回答道，“这重要吗？”

“这些只是例行的问题，”埃利奥特说，“那么，您到家之后做了什么？”

“我先打开行李取出东西，然后洗澡，”她说，“然后我又尝试给亚历克斯拨电话，这一点如果你们已经查了他的电话答录机你们就会知道。”

“格兰特小姐，您有移动电话吗？”埃利奥特问道。

“当然，”她回答道，“但是我没有用它给亚历克斯打电话，如果您是要问这个的话。我用的是那边的那部电话。”

埃利奥特忽然觉得高兴起来。她说的话将很容易核实。机场的停车场将能够告诉他们她是什么时候离开的，而电话公司会有她的电话记录。如果她是从家里打的电话，那就不可能是她杀的福尔利。在那种交通状况下，她再早也不可能在 3 点 20 分之前到达他家。而且她也肯定不会在 3 点 45 分之前再回到自己家里。这一次，他竟感谢这样的交通状况。

## 第97页

在车里鲍恩没有说话，埃利奥特知道他在和自己生气。那天早上他看到她的时候，竟然忘记问她手机的事了。不过那也只会节约一点点时间，比他们在克劳瑟夫妇身上浪费掉的时间少得多。

回到警察局，鲍恩只用了二十分钟就核实了阿曼达的叙述。她在爱丁堡的一个同事开车送她到机场，飞机在两点零五分到达，正如她说的那样。停车场和电话公司都给出了与她所说相符的信息。

“这么看来好像她也没有犯罪，”埃利奥特说道，“并且她是得到他所有财产的那个人。我们刚刚和他的律师谈过了，好像福尔利在两周前立下遗嘱，把一切都留给了她。但是我不敢说她会有多高兴。她似乎并没有对他的钱感到很心安理得。”

难道这个案子真的有它看起来那样不一般吗？金钱或爱情是警察不得不处理的大部分案件的根源，并且与二者都有关的案件也有很多。他感觉这二者肯定与亚历克斯·福尔利的死亡都有点儿关联，但是他没能发现关联是什么。他正发现越来越多的人都有杀害福尔利的理由，但是他们又好像都没有下手的机会。

## 第98页

埃利奥特他们去跟莉萨·维尔弗交谈，但是并不指望她会告诉他们什么有用的信息。他开始倾向于认为亚历克斯·福尔利终究是自杀。

那天晚间，埃利奥特的话比平时要少一些，虽然他总是尽量不把工作状态带回家。因为他的工作而使家人受折磨是不公平的。他尽力去听米基讲的一个关于他同学的冗长故事。但是埃利奥特还是感觉到这个案子有什么地方不对劲。他相信自己的感觉，但是他没有太多时间。

“所以后来保罗打了戴维一拳，然后托马斯小姐让他自己独坐了半个小时。我很高兴他揍了他。”米基说着。

“但你不应该打人。”埃利奥特不假思索地说。

“是的，但是您知道戴维做了什么吗，爸爸？他告诉保罗托马斯小姐给我们留了五页作业，其实她一页都没给我们留。”

“他为什么撒那样的谎呢？”埃利奥特尽量表现得感兴趣。

“保罗把他的钢笔弄坏了，所以他生他气了。您知道保罗花了多长时间做作业吗？两个半小时呢。何况他讨厌数学。难道戴维不招人恨吗？爸爸！您在干什么？把我放下！”

## 第99页

埃利奥特一把抱起他不知所措的儿子，带着他在厨房里跳起舞来。

“谢谢你啦，米基，”他说，“我现在明白了。你的故事帮了大忙。”

埃利奥特刚才突然明白他忽略了什么。现在他觉得他知道福尔利发生了什么，但是在他能够确定之前，还有事情需要他去查验一下，而且他还得让鲍恩读完福尔利的日记。

# 第 18 章　真相大白

## 第100页

“但是您为什么把我带到这里来？”维尔弗医生问道，“我很忙。”

埃利奥特选了最宽敞、装修最漂亮的一间讯问室。墙壁刚刚粉刷过，家具也都是新的。他要让维尔弗感到放松。

“哦，我们只是再需要一点儿信息，”埃利奥特说道，“这完全是例行公事，并且我们想把这次谈话录下来。您不会介意的，对吗，先生？”

维尔弗摇了摇头，然后埃利奥特打开了盒式磁带录音机的开关。

“现在您能再讲一下您和福尔利先生最后一次见面的情形吗？”他问道。

维尔弗重复了他们上次见面时他告诉他们的内容。起初他似乎很紧张，好像在等埃利奥特说话。但是他很快开始放松了。埃利奥特认真地听着，并且时不时地点点头。

“谢谢您，先生，”维尔弗说完以后他礼貌地说，“那么现在，您能再跟我们说说他去世的那天下午您在哪里吗？当然这也仅仅是例行公事。我们得询问每一个人。”

## 第101页

维尔弗更加放松了。

“好的，没问题，虽然昨天我都跟刑侦警员鲍恩讲过了。整个下午我都在诊所里，很多人看到我了。我很奇怪你们竟然没有问过他们，督察先生。但是可能你们也太忙了。”

他冲埃利奥特微笑着，但是在听到埃利奥特接下来的一个问题后，他的笑容开始消失了。

“维尔弗医生，您是什么时候把福尔利先生的检查结果给他的？”

“我告诉过您，星期四晚上我打电话告诉他的。您可以通过电话公司核实一下。”

“那么您是什么时候从医院拿到检查结果的，先生？”埃利奥特问道。

维尔弗医生把目光移开了。

“大概在周四早上，”他说，“但是很难记得准了。”

“甚至当这个病人是一个好朋友，而且非常担心检查结果的时候也记不准吗？”埃利奥特问道。

“恐怕是这样的，督察先生。我们每天会拿到那么多检查结果。”维尔弗说。

一行汗水出现在他的前额上。

“好吧，让我来帮助您回忆一下，”他说，“医院在星期一的早上就打电话把检查结果给您了。现在，您能告诉我们为什么您等了这么长时间才把它们交给福尔利先生吗？”

## 第103页

这位医生用手帕擦干了额头。

“我只是忘记了，”他说，“上个星期我每天都很忙。”

“但是还没忙到不能在周五去看看福尔利的程度。不，我不相信是那样的。我认为您有很充分的理由要让这些结果不为人知，维尔弗医生。”

“您是什么意思啊？”这位医生问道。

“我想您知道我是什么意思，”埃利奥特说，“您在星期四给福尔利打电话的时候，我认为您没有告诉他检查结果。我认为您是告诉他您需要一些钱，想卖掉一些东西。这就是为什么他带那么多现金回家。然后周五去看他的时候，您在他的检查结果上撒了谎。您告诉他他长了个脑部肿瘤。您知道如果检查结果表明他有肿瘤他就打算自杀，这一点他已经和您讨论过了。还有，您也知道他有克劳瑟的枪。”

“我不知道您在说什么，”维尔弗说，“亚历克斯从来没有和我讨论过自杀的事。如果他提到过，我肯定会告诉他不要那样做。我是一名医生，而且我还是他的朋友。我会有什么理由那么做呢？您电视剧看多了，督察先生。”

## 第104页

“理由就是您的妻子，莉萨，”埃利奥特说，“您知道他和福尔利先生有私情，并且您知道她想离开您和他在一起。您不能允许那样的事情发生，对吧，先生？我们有福尔利先生的日记。我们知道关于这段感情的所有事情，并且我们知道他告诉过您他自杀的计划。”

一提到日记，维尔弗的脸似乎没了血色。他把头埋到了手心里。长长的一段沉默。当他开始说话时，埃利奥特和鲍恩不得不倾身向前去听他在说什么。

“亚历克斯从来不需要为任何事奋斗，”他说，“他有他想要的一切。但是他不能把莉萨带走，我不会让萨姆像我一样在没有妈妈的家里长大。为了我所得到的一切，我已经奋斗得如此辛苦了。我不会让任何人把这些从我这里带走。您说对了，督察先生。亚历克斯是个脆弱的人。我知道他如果长了脑瘤的话就没法活下去，所以我让他以为自己可能长了脑瘤。他没有意识到那是我的暗示。我甚至劝他把枪弄干净，这样在枪上就不会有指纹。这件事真简单，太简单了。”

他看了埃利奥特一会儿。

“可笑的是，莉莎还是离开了我。”他说着，声音里似乎带着笑声。

## 第105页

“您告诉他您想卖掉的是什么东西，医生？”埃利奥特平静地问道。

“我起居室里的镜子。它是我拥有的最漂亮的东西。”

他看了埃利奥特一会儿。

“我没想到您会察觉出来，督察先生，”他微笑着说，“您看上去不是特别聪明的样子。”

埃利奥特没有回应。

在被带到牢房之前，维尔弗又问了一个问题。

“萨姆现在该怎么办？”他说，但是他似乎并没有指望得到答案。

埃利奥特感到非常疲倦。他很高兴这个案子结了。他已经见够了福尔利的朋友了，除了阿曼达·格兰特。这次讯问让他回味起来极不舒服。像维尔弗这样的男人坚信他们可以掌控一切。他怎么会真就认为福尔利的死能解决他儿子的问题？特别是萨姆还那么喜爱福尔利。埃利奥特为这个男孩儿感到很难过。他知道维尔弗实际上只在考虑他自己。爱可以如此盲目，他想。

他朝房间的那边看过去。鲍恩在埋头看笔记，深色卷发盖住了他的黑眼圈。他昨晚通宵读完了福尔利的日记。埃利奥特暗自微微一笑。他想知道鲍恩要犹豫多久才会给琳达·斯科特打电话。她会有时间吗？她会对他感兴趣吗？这次他可能会走运，埃利奥特希望是这样，但是在生活中你永远无法说得准任何事情。